My Beautiful Struggle

My Beautiful Struggle

JORDAN BONE

with Cathryn Kemp

The right of Jordan Bone to be identified as the author
of this work has been asserted in accordance with
the Copyright, Designs and Patents Act 1988.

This edition first published in Great Britain in 2017 by
Trapeze
an imprint of the Orion Publishing Group Ltd
Carmelite House
50 Victoria Embankment
London EC4Y 0DZ
An Hachette UK Company

1 3 5 7 9 10 8 6 4 2

A CIP catalogue record for this book
is available from the British Library.

ISBN: 978 1 4091 7152 2

Typeset by Input Data Services Ltd, Somerset

Printed and bound by CPI Group (UK) Ltd, Croydon, CR0 4YY

Contents

Prologue

I wish you could have seen my daughter as a young girl, full of hope, full of laughter and life. She was always beautiful. I know every mother says that, but Jordan had something special, a twinkle in her eye, a cheeky smile, a giggle that was hard to suppress.

Imagine for one brief moment that you knew her. That she was the girl next door, an angel lighting up every room she went into. She was the little girl with blonde waves who refused to wear jeans, who even wore her Disney Belle dress in bed at night, and who was so thrilled to become a bridesmaid at the age of three that she wore the dress for weeks afterwards! Each night I would lie next to my baby girl, telling her story after story until she snuggled down next to me, her breathing becoming heavier, her eyelashes fluttering as she sank into her dreams of castles and fairies.

Imagine watching her grow up; her kind nature, her love of singing and dance. When the film *Titanic* came out, she role-played with her friends for months, creating little dance routines and singing her heart out. Then, at the age of eleven, she became a big sister and was so thrilled. She was so proud of Eden, and would smother her in cuddles.

With each passing year Jordan was blossoming into a lovely young woman.

Then imagine how you would have felt hearing the news. The news that every parent dreads: that your child has been involved in a car accident. It is a moment made of pure ice; a moment of shock that reverberates for years to come. It is horror and it is fear in their purest forms.

On 7 May 2005, I was that mother. I received a call from one of my fifteen-year-old daughter's friends. She was in hysterics, babbling something about a car crash, saying that Jordan was trapped, and to 'come quick'. I didn't have time to react. I think I may have dropped the phone, but things got a bit hazy with shock. I grabbed my house keys and a thin jacket, but all the time I was thinking *She's dead – I've lost her*. The world stopped turning. My breathing felt slow and sluggish, though I was probably panting like a dog with fear. I screamed at my partner Darren to take us there. I had to bring Eden with us – she was only three – I couldn't leave her.

My limbs felt like they were moving through thick treacle, yet somehow I made it to the place where the accident had happened, in a country lane in King's Lynn. All the while I was thinking, *But she said she was going to Tesco. She's nowhere near Tesco.* It was as if my mind had got stuck on that puzzle and I could think of nothing else. Time became elastic, expanding and contracting as I kept going forward through the echoes of my worst nightmare.

I couldn't say how long it took me to reach the scene, or how long I stayed there. I grabbed Eden and ran towards the carnage. I remember raw grief burning my heart, stinging tears in my eyes. I remember the sight of all those flashing lights. The ambulance. The paramedics in their green uniforms. The police officers redirecting traffic away from that road where my girl lay.

I can't remember what I said to the officers; my voice was constricted, my throat tight, and there seemed to be no words that were adequate. I didn't listen to their responses. I kept moving, so slowly, so quickly, running at full pelt, Eden clinging to me, towards the car that had its wheels in the air. The world had turned over, literally.

That boy, the one who had only just passed his test, was standing on the roadside. He may even have been smoking a cigarette. I barely glanced at him. I knelt down by the windscreen, my knees crunching on the glass that lay in shards across the ditch, among the leaves and twigs and debris from the crash. I called Jordan's name, expecting no response. I thought she was dead. I thought she had died.

I was already cold to the bone, though it was a mild,

showery May day, at the thought that I'd lost my blonde angel, the light of my life along with her little sister Eden. I can't remember if I prayed. I'm not a believer; never have been one for religion and all that. Yet of course in times like these it is usual, expected even, to pray for the right outcome, to ask a deity, long ignored, to intercede. I don't think I did. I don't think I could do anything. I was frozen inside, absolutely sure I'd lost her for good.

Suddenly, I wanted to be dead too.

Then I heard it.

A thin, reedy voice was singing a popular chart song. It was coming from inside the car. It was Jordan, my Jordan, and she was singing. Singing was always her 'thing'. One of her favourite presents one Christmas as a child – I think she was nine years old – was a microphone. She belted out hit after hit, driving the neighbours mad and keeping her family entertained. There was one song by Céline Dion, 'My Heart Will Go On', that she was mad about.

When she was approaching the age of ten it was all about the Spice Girls. 'Baby' was her favourite. I remember she always begged me to put her long blonde hair in two bunches like Emma Bunton's every morning to wear to school. At primary school, when she and her friends pretended to be the Spice Girls, practising the song and dance routines, she was always Baby Spice. My sister and I even took her to Earls Court to see the band, her golden hair plaited all over, which took ages to do. I can still picture the joy on her face as the singers appeared on stage.

I guess I always knew that if Jordan was singing, it meant she was OK. She was irrepressible, a force of nature even as a child, though she was sweet and shy underneath.

So hearing her voice was a magical moment amid the horror of that day, not just because it meant she was alive. It meant she was still 'herself' in there, with whatever injuries she had sustained.

'Mum, Mum, is that you?' Jordan stopped singing. I peered into the space where the windscreen was, and there she was, lying on her front. She was living and breathing and talking to me.

My heart swooped. My mind freaked out. I think I was shouting. I turned to Tim, who'd been driving the car, and had a real go at him, calling him 'irresponsible' and 'reckless'. It was Jordan herself who stopped me!

'For God's sake, Mother, calm down!' Jordan's voice was stronger.

I turned back, my attention instantly focused on her. I tried to hold her hand but couldn't quite reach. Jordan was lying on the roof of the car, which had landed on the floor of the rain-splattered ditch. There was blood everywhere. Her hair was soaked red with it, but she looked like she was OK. Her beautiful face was unaltered.

I felt so helpless, I couldn't even stroke her hand to reassure her.

'Oh my God, Jordan, you gave me such a fright. I thought . . .' I was gabbling. My head was spinning; I started to shake. I was trying to hold it together for Jordan's sake, but to be honest, I was failing badly.

'Calm down, Mum.' Jordan's voice was croaky. 'I'm paralysed.'

'You're what? Don't be silly, you're not *paralysed*, Jordan. You're going to be fine.'

I dismissed her, thinking it was the shock of the accident talking. How could she be disabled when she could sing and speak?

'Mum, I just know. I'm paralysed. I can't feel anything.'

At that moment, a paramedic pushed me gently aside.

'We need to work here,' was all he said. I nodded in response, consoled but anxious.

'She says she's paralysed.' I looked up into his face, a face I cannot remember, smeared by the nightmarish quality of the day.

'It's probably shock – don't worry too much at this stage.'

He told me to wait at the end of the lane. My heart was now racing as if I was having a heart attack.

'Just settle down, be calm,' I said to myself. 'She's alive, she's still with us.'

Though I was scared for Jordan, though I knew she was being cut out of the vehicle while I paced up and down the lane, I still thought everything would be OK. How naive I was! How desperately, stupidly, utterly naive. Nothing would ever be the same again. Our lives were about to change in the most profound way possible. None of us would come out of this unscathed. Jordan would go through hell. It would take years for any kind of 'normality' to be restored. Yet she was alive, and what was more important than that?

Today I look at my beautiful daughter, the one who tottered down the street in heels wanting desperately to look like she was in the film *Legally Blonde*, and I feel that this young woman who has been through so much is no longer the girl I gave birth to.

She is not the baby I watched take her first faltering steps; the toddler who ran over to me in the park; the child who skipped in and out of her paddling pool in the garden. That young girl, who turned into a kind, warm, caring teenager and who loved dancing with her friends, was struck down in a heartbeat. She was struck down in her prime. Her life was altered irrevocably, and her strength of character was tested to its very limits.

Jordan was taken to the very edge of what is possible to cope with as a human being. Yet it seemed to me that her spirit never faltered, even when mine was vanquished.

I remember weeks later, after the operation to repair her broken neck, I walked down the length of the hospital corridor towards her room, knowing that Jordan may not have survived the dangerous procedure. I knew that even if she had survived, she could be altered again: she could lose her voice, when she had lost so much already, or her terrible injuries could be made even worse by the intervention of well-meaning surgeons. As I walked through the hospital that day, I had no hope left – I'd used all mine up. I was preparing for the worst.

Then I saw her face, her determination, and I realised that while her body was broken, her spirit was not . . .

1

Barefaced

Me, Uncovered

'The unachievable is achievable.'

Hey, guys, I hope you're all well. I always start off my vlogs like this, and so it feels right to do the same in my book!

Wow, I can't believe I'm writing an *actual* book, and that you guys want to read it! It's such a privilege to share my story.

If you follow my blog on Bloglovin, or are a subscriber to my YouTube channel, you'll know that when I was just fifteen I was in a bad car accident and broke my neck at the C6 level. That means I've been paralysed from the chest down ever since. I can't feel anything below my décolletage – there's no sensation at all. It goes without saying that I can't walk. I've had to retrain my body to be able to sit upright, building up the strength during those torturous hours in hospital, and I can only do that because I had a major operation on my neck to rebuild it (more about that later!).

My arms have some mobility, so I can use them to help me put on my make-up, but my hands have no movement at all. My fingers are permanently crunched together. I do have some movement in my wrists, as you'll know if you've seen any of my beauty tutorials online. This movement was the key to my being able to relearn to apply products, though it took a long, long time and loads of perseverance (and many failures!) to get to the point I'm at today where I can create whatever make-up look I want, and even teach you guys to do it too!

I can move my head and my neck, though I get pretty achy in the tops of my shoulders and at the point where my neck and spine meet. I often have to shift position, or put a warm comforter round my neck to keep me cosy and relax the muscles. I use a wheelchair all the time, except when I'm in bed, of course, and I'm able to push myself, though I still get tired quite easily.

My new home has been built especially for me, and I can glide through the wide corridors and get about really easily, which is great. My favourite room in the house is my beauty room. All of you who have watched my recent vlogs will have seen it, with my silver-motifed wallpaper and white walls. It's my haven; truly my sanctuary. I have a huge make-up desk and a mirror with lights round it. I have drawers literally rammed with products – seriously, they are chock-full of all the amazing things I get sent to try out and review for you guys out there. I couldn't begin to count them, but I guess I've got 500 lipsticks, maybe 50 foundations, drawers filled with hundreds of eyeshadow palettes, countless mascaras, pomades, creams, lip stains and gloss.

There are all my artfully arranged white pots stuffed full of gorgeous brushes, lined up on my table. It's every girl's (and perhaps some boys' . . .?) dream beauty room – well, it's definitely mine, at least! And I now have my dream job – trialling make-up, speaking about motivation and positive thinking and going to glamorous events, even being whisked away to New York by a global beauty brand!

But most importantly, I get to speak to you guys, sharing my tips for a better and brighter 'you' and cheering you on from the digital sidelines. I've always been a 'girly' girl, into my Barbies and dressing up in fashionable clothes, so having all this fills me with utter delight. It's a true expression of my identity.

This is who I am, and seeing it every day reminds me how far I've come to achieve all this. It hasn't been easy. There have been major challenges and upsets along the way. I live with a big disability, and so everyday life can still be difficult, and my book will show you what I have been thinking on my journey back from the accident to becoming who I am meant to be.

I've always been very fussy about my hair. I know exactly how I like it styled – big and bouncy! I love a good blow-dry – and that has been one of the difficulties, finding a carer who is good at doing hair, because Mum, who used to do it, is pretty rubbish! I don't think she'd mind me saying that. That sounds like a minor difficulty when you think about everything else I need help with, but beauty is not just about looking good – to me, it's about *feeling* good. Make-up, clothes and hair became the focus of my search for my own identity growing up, and again after the accident, and so it's natural that I like them to be right, to reflect who I am and what I stand for. Some people are surprised that I still make as much effort with my looks as I used to. But why wouldn't I? Wheelchair users like myself are invisible enough, except when people stare. There's no way I was ever going to disappear behind my disability. It's not who I am. I was never going to cower away.

In fact, I've been determined to stand out from the crowd despite my paralysis. I want to show you guys that no matter what your situation, your disability or your attitude, you can change and make the best of yourself and your life, just as I have done.

The harsh reality for me is that my life continues to be something that has to be planned around being paralysed. No amount of positive thinking changes my physical limitations!

I need twenty-four-hour, round-the-clock help from my

carers. At 8.30 a.m. the first carer comes in to help me get up. I can't dress myself, make my breakfast, fetch a drink or even get myself into my own wheelchair. Everything has to be done by others, including washing me, which I find pretty undignified – but I'm not a negative person so I choose not to dwell on that too much. It takes a full hour and a half to get me ready to face the day, and that's before I've put my make-up on!

During the day my carer helps with normal tasks, such as making lunch, getting me drinks and checking I'm OK, but these days they also set up my tripod and lights, making sure the camera angle is right, switching on the camera and leaving me to film my videos.

Later, the carer leaves at around 5 p.m., then at 9.30 p.m. the night carer comes in and helps me undress, wash and get into bed. She has to stay through the night, as I have to be turned at least every three hours to stop sore patches from forming on my body. It means I don't get much uninterrupted sleep – another good reason for using loads of concealer to hide the dark circles under my eyes!

Privacy is a luxury, and I don't get much of it, but as I said, I'm not a complainer. I prefer to get on with things, as you'll hopefully see in these pages!

Obviously things weren't always this way. My life changed dramatically on the day of my accident, but I'd faced and overcome challenges before then. Being someone who believes in herself hasn't always been easy, even before my injury. I've been through bullying and the loneliness it brings; depression and, of course, the terrible crash that changed my life forever, but I always felt I was destined to do something out of the ordinary.

Even as a young girl I wanted to be 'somebody', and all through my troubles I always knew I would be successful one day, as long as I kept going, kept believing in myself and kept feeling I had something to offer.

Immediately before the crash, I had come through months of being bullied by girls at school who I had known for years. I know that thousands of people can relate to how that feels! Despite the pain it gave me, I always tried to hold my head high. I wouldn't give them the satisfaction of knowing how deeply they were hurting me, and how confused I was by their sudden change in feelings towards me. I was upset, but I held onto something more precious: my dignity. Every day was awful, going into school, feeling like I was a social pariah. I would feel sick as I entered the school gates, but I turned it around.

I kept going in. I kept facing up to it, showing them I wasn't beaten. Over time, I made lots of new friends in Year Ten. At that point I was fifteen, had an amazing social life and had discovered in myself an absolute passion for beauty and fashion. Things felt great again.

I had my whole life ahead of me, and yet that was the

point at which everything fell apart, a million times worse than before.

That hopeful, happy teenage girl was in for a shock beyond imagining. All those dreams and hopes, ambitions and joys were ripped from me because of the crash, and what was worse, as I lay there face down on the ceiling of the car that had rolled over, I knew it. I knew that everything would be different; that simple joys like paddling in the sea, the waves lapping against my feet, the shock of cold, wet sand squelching between my toes, would be forever denied me. I knew I'd never again kick my way through crisp autumn leaves, dodge puddles or truly feel the embrace of someone special. Call it instinct, or a sixth sense, but I knew I was paralysed. Yet I had no idea to what extent it would affect me and my family.

Fast-forward twelve years, and I've turned my life around 360 degrees, and in more ways than you can imagine.

Through a combination of sheer willpower, meditation and positive thinking, I decided I *would* be successful, I *would* make a difference, I *would* live my live to the fullest it could possibly be.

I've always done my best to turn negative experiences into positive ones. I don't know if I was born that way, or if at some point I consciously made a choice within myself to try and live the best life I could. As a child I was really shy and would hide behind Mum's legs if people tried to talk to me, but as I grew older, and as my interest was sparked for fashion and beauty, I began to feel good in my own skin, so perhaps that is when I thought, 'You know what, I'm only here once, so I'm going to make sure I do what feels good to me.' It's a simple philosophy, but one that has got me where I am today: a global beauty vlogger with a following of hundreds of thousands across the world. Every time I see the numbers my eyes pop – 186,000 YouTube subscribers, 127,000 Instagram followers, 12,000 Twitter followers and 165,000 Facebook followers!

In so many ways my beauty blogging saved my life.

Nowadays brands approach me – can you believe that?! People listen to my opinion; they rate what I have to say. I can hardly believe it myself, when you think that twelve years ago I couldn't even clutch a mascara wand, my injuries were so severe.

I'm writing this book to inspire you, to let you know that you can achieve anything, against even the greatest of odds. We all have pain in life that can hold us back, but we have the choice too to let it break us or make us.

If I can push myself to relearn how to apply make-up without hands that move and with limited movement in my arms; if I can go from a girl with sadness and resentment, and, let's face it, a big bundle of self-pity, to a woman with passion, drive and self-belief, then so can you.

Today I feel like the luckiest girl alive. I love my fiancé Mike so much. I have two crazy dogs: one chihuahua, Lola, and one Pomeranian cross, Pumpkin. I have a wonderful, supportive family and close friends too. I feel so fortunate to have these people around me.

Yet it could have been so different. I could've given up and lived half a life, away from the spotlight, spending the rest of my days eaten up with anger or sadness for what happened to me. I wouldn't have blamed myself if I did! What happened to me was a nightmare. I did go through hell. There were dark times, when I wasn't sure I even wanted to live any more. But I got through it, as you can too. I refused to lie down and give up. That's so not me! I'm a fighter. I'm a survivor, but most of all I like to think of myself now as a 'thrive-r'!

I'm living a life I could barely have imagined, even as a non-disabled teenager. In *My Beautiful Struggle* I will take you through my journey, both personal and beauty-ful, laying bare my experiences and feelings. It is like being barefaced, before my make-up is applied, exposing myself as I really am with no disguise, no trickery, no cover-ups at all. Without shame. This is me, as I am. I'm the same 'Jordan' as the glamorous woman behind the camera. What you see is no different, but in this I take you deeper, through my hard times, sharing what got me through, what helped me to achieve what I have today.

I'll also share the knowledge I've gained about applying make-up to make you *look* great, and the tips I've learnt about keeping positive to make you *feel* great. I'll show you that the unachievable can become the achievable; the impossible, the possible. I found my strength in beauty and positivity, and now it's up to you to find out what empowers you to change the way you live and feel. Join me on my journey of inner and outer beauty.

2

Primer

Starting Over

'We cannot choose our circumstances, or what happens to us, but we can choose how to face them.'

'Hey, Tim, hey, Jamie! Wow, is that your car?' A silver Citroën Saxo had pulled over and stopped at the kerbside as my friend Sarah and I walked down the road. We were heading for the Tesco store to stock up on snacks and drinks for a sleepover that night. Sarah was my friend from round the corner. We went to different schools but hung out together a lot at weekends. She was a year younger than me, and a little taller with brown shoulder-length hair. We both loved the same things: clothes, shopping and being sociable. That day we'd met up in my street and were chatting away as we made our way to the superstore.

I didn't know it, but that would be the last time I ever walked.

Two minutes after we started our mooch together, a car drew up.

'Hey, girls, how's it going?' said Tim, the seventeen-year-old driver. He was leaning over the other boy in the car, Jamie, fourteen, his younger brother, to speak to us, the passenger window wound down. We both knew Jamie from the area; he was in Sarah's year at school, so she knew him better than I did, and we'd heard on the grapevine that his brother had just passed his driving test.

'We're good, thanks,' replied Sarah, peering into the vehicle. She looked a little awestruck by Tim and his car. 'It's so cool you can drive now.'

'Yeah, it's amazing,' answered Tim, running his hand through his dark, wet-look, spiked-up hair, laughing over his brother who was also grinning at us. 'Why don't you girls hop in? Let's go for a spin!'

Tim nudged Jamie, who had the same hairstyle, only ginger, and the boys both snorted at some private joke, hitting the knuckles of a single closed fist together in a gesture of unleashed masculinity. Jamie opened his door and jumped out, standing on the kerb beside us. The car only had two doors and so we would have to climb inside.

I turned to Sarah and we shared a look. It seemed that we were both thinking it might not be a good idea – we had no idea if Tim was going to drive safely. I wanted to say something, but I didn't want to appear stupid or scared in front of the boys.

Sarah looked back at me. She appeared hesitant as well. Neither of us had expected this to happen.

At that point Jamie leant against the bonnet with feigned indolence. Both boys were wearing T-shirts, jeans and trendy trainers. They were into rap music, and it was blaring through the speakers.

'Come on, it'll be a laugh; we've got some good sounds. We can cruise around, see who's about. It'll be fun,' Tim called from the driver's seat.

Sarah and I both laughed, probably to hide any doubt we had about the wisdom of getting into a car with an inexperienced driver.

I looked at her and shrugged. 'Oh, why not? Might be a laugh,' I said.

'OK,' she agreed.

It had been a strange day, bright sunshine one minute, pelting down with rain the next. It looked like another shower was starting, and at least this way we weren't going to get soaked.

I don't know why I did it. I look back and cannot think what possessed me. Mum had always told me never to get in a car with men I didn't know, or boys that maybe I did! It was considered quite a 'skanky' thing to do, which meant it wasn't very classy. It was a bit cheap, and I'd always considered myself one of the girls who didn't go about getting into boys' cars, even though that makes me sound a bit snobby. But it was true! I didn't even know Tim that well, but at the same time I didn't have any reason to think we wouldn't be safe. He had passed his test. That meant he should be a competent driver, surely?

I nodded my response. I wasn't convinced, though, and even at the door of the car, as both Sarah and I made to get in, I hesitated. Then we both went to get in at the same time; we laughed as we bumped into each other, so I signalled for Sarah to get in first, not wanting to look foolish. Sarah climbed in and sat behind the driver's seat. I followed, sitting behind Jamie, who climbed back into the passenger seat.

That moment of indecision became the base on which the rest of my life is now fixed. If I had got in first, then who knows; I may have walked free from the crash, just as Sarah and the others did. That single split second almost cost me my life.

We put our seat belts on. I glanced over at Sarah, sitting beside me. She mirrored my own unease but we managed to smile.

'Let's go!' Tim indicated then pulled away from the kerb on Gaywood Road where he'd stopped to speak to us. We were soon moving past familiar streets. Inside, the vehicle was plastered with some kind of fake Louis Vuitton or Gucci upholstery.

50 Cent's 'Candy Shop' was playing on the stereo.

Tim wasn't driving too fast and so I started to relax,

thinking that perhaps this could be a laugh after all. We weren't in a hurry to go anywhere except the supermarket, but we'd already driven past it as neither of us had mentioned that's where we were heading. I began to think it might be cool to hang out with an older boy.

But then things changed.

Tim spotted some lads driving a car behind us. It sounded like he knew them. He reached over and turned up the music, the track pumping out as he accelerated, saying, 'Let's lose them.'

The car seemed to get faster and faster. The music sounded louder and louder. I looked to my left and saw a man walking his dog. The simple freedom and normality of it struck me. I realised I wanted to get out of this car. I wanted to be walking, even getting wet in the rain – anything rather than be in this speeding 'tin can' right now. We stopped at a set of traffic lights. Instead of taking the left turn, which would've taken us in a loop back to mine, Tim went straight on ahead.

I think that was the moment I felt the most powerless.

There was little traffic on the roads, and the familiar streets of King's Lynn rushed past us now as Tim urged the car on, thumping the steering wheel for emphasis while Jamie moved his head to the beat of the music.

By now the car was going way too fast, and it was scaring me.

Slow down, Tim, please just let me out, I screamed inside

my head. *Why the hell did I get into the car? I feel so bloody stupid!* Despite my internal pleading, I still didn't have the courage to beg him to pull over, but perhaps he wouldn't have listened to me if I had.

Panic rose within me. Trees raced past us out of the window. I froze, my mind whirling with fear, holding onto the seat with both hands gripped tightly to the edge of the faux designer cladding. My heart was pounding.

Please, just stop, just stop and let me out. He has to get fed up of driving, doesn't he? I whispered to myself. I couldn't have made him hear me even if I'd tried, as the beat of the rap music blared from the car stereo. Sarah and I shot terrified looks at each other. By now, we knew this wasn't going to end well. I could see that from the expression on Sarah's face, reflecting mine. We grabbed for each other's hands. There was no time to pray, but then who or what would I have prayed to? It felt like we were beyond help, beyond divine intervention of any sort. I wasn't brought up to be religious, preferring to trust in my own sense of my destiny rather than a great force somewhere out there deciding my fate. Yet it had got me here, inside this car, speeding towards an unknown future, my fate already sealed, though I didn't yet know it.

The car's wheels bumped as they hit Castle Rising Road, which was more like a country lane. We'd only been driving a few minutes. Everything happened so quickly. It wasn't raining but there were gaping great puddles in the road from earlier. The car swerved as it hit one of them, speeding through the rainwater.

It was all over in a fraction of a second.

The moment when my life, as it was, was utterly destroyed; altered forever.

The car aquaplaned. Tim took his hands from the steering wheel, holding them aloft in a kind of quasi-religious pose. Jamie grabbed for the wheel as the car spun out of control, veering violently to the right. The trees reared up in front of us. The lane was dark, bushes and vegetation covering both sides of the road completely.

My next thought was, *we're going to die.*

The last thing I remember is the screaming as the world turned over along with the car, which landed in a ditch at the roadside, the radio still blaring.

Then there was silence. I think perhaps I had passed out. The crash, even now, is a blur of noises, people and lucid moments interwoven with panic, fear and the strange sensation of having no sensations at all.

Blinking, my eyes focused but I wrinkled my face, confused. Where was the steering wheel? Where were the passengers? Why was I facing what looked like a ditch, and several tree stumps? It was then I realised that I was lying on my front on the inside of the roof of the car, facing through the back window, which was the wrong way up. I'd been flipped over.

I could hear voices from the roadside; I was sure there

was no one else inside the vehicle with me. It was then that I felt the pain in my neck, an agony I can barely describe.

'Call an ambulance,' I said with as much strength as I could manage. Sarah's knees appeared, crouching next to me. 'Call Mum,' I added. My throat tightened and I felt rather than saw that the seat belt was twisted around my neck, strangling me as I hung from it. Panic set in. My weight was pulling down on the seat belt, which was now tightening with every breath I took.

'Help me, I'm choking, I can't breathe!' I managed to shout and one of the boys, Tim, I think, peered into the back. His face was white with shock. It seemed obvious, even to me in the state I was in, that no one knew what the hell to do.

'Undo the seat belt, I can't breathe,' I said again, wondering why everyone was so slow to act. My heart was thudding as adrenalin coursed through me. The car seemed to swim yellow in front of my eyes, and I knew I was seconds from passing out.

I don't know how he did it but moments later, or so it seemed, he returned. I was drowning, in and out of consciousness, then I felt the sudden jolt of relief as the seat belt, my hangman's noose, was undone.

Perhaps that was the point at which my neck was broken. Perhaps that was the moment that continues to define every second of my existence. Who can ever know?

My head snapped forward and I slumped onto the car

roof. Lying there, my face and hair covered with glass from the shattered windscreen, I was surrounded by a pool of blood that I realised by now was probably mine. But I was grateful to be able to gasp in lungfuls of air. Still alive. Still breathing.

Thoughts drifted in and out. Why did the back window have no glass? Had someone rung the ambulance? Out of nowhere a memory popped into my head of a traumatic experience in my otherwise happy childhood. I was sitting in my Nanno's parked car, putting my seat belt on. Mum had come out of the vet's. Our cat Willow had been put down and, being distressed, Mum didn't look where she was going. A car appeared out of nowhere and knocked her over, sending her body flying into the air. I felt like that small girl again. Peering out of the car window, seeing my mum slump to the ground, watching as people ran over, then the police arriving. I screamed 'Mum!' from the car, convinced she was dead, but she wasn't. She actually stood up and walked away. To this day she says it was the padded bag slung round her body that saved her, stopped her from hitting the concrete road. I don't know why it came into my head now.

Perhaps it was the irony. Perhaps it was the trauma. But this time it was me who had been thrown through the air, and I knew deep down that I wouldn't be getting up and walking away, ever again.

An eternity passed, or perhaps it was a few minutes. The world started to go dark around me, my eyes rolled back in their sockets and a strange peace overcame me. Even the pain in my neck seemed to vanish, and I remember thinking I could get used to that lack of feeling.

Something like peace or serenity washed over me. Then there was light, a strong light that shone through the darkness in my mind, and the temptation to follow that light, to keep feeling that calm, was overwhelming.

But my conscious mind had other ideas. With an injection of pure adrenalin I realised I had to stay awake. I had a strong sense that if I drifted towards that light, with its promise of peace, then perhaps that was the way towards dying; perhaps that would be the end.

I objected to dying at that moment, even though I think I knew deep down even then that something was profoundly different about me. My will to survive was so strong that I knew I had to do something to keep myself awake. I had too much to live for: my kid sister Eden, my mum and the rest of my family; my passion for beauty and fashion, singing and acting.

I was so young. I had plans, ambitions, goals and dreams. For God's sake, I had things I wanted to do with my life, and they didn't include dying in a cold, murky ditch at the roadside! Death just wasn't an option, so when I saw that light I knew I had to battle harder than I ever had before in order to stay alive.

In a thin, small voice I sang the song 'You've Got The Love' in a whisper, repeating the same few lines over and over. *Sometimes it seems the going is just too rough / And things go wrong no matter what I do / Now and then it seems that life is just too much / But you've got the love I need to see me through* . . . The words felt like a mantra, a way of keeping myself motivated to stay awake. They made sense to me at the time anyway.

As I sang my breath came in jerky, panicking spasms. I knew that this was a fight for my life, and one I now desperately wanted to win. If I'd known then the level of my disability, would I have clung to life so passionately? I have asked myself this question in my darker moments, expecting to hesitate or defer the question for more positive times, but the answer has always been, unequivocally, yes.

Yes, I was left paralysed from the chest down, though I was yet to understand that. Yes, I was facing a life so very different to the one I should have been leading. But yes – despite all that, I always, always have hope that things can be better, that life does get better, no matter what happens. So I guess it was sheer optimism that pulled me through those minutes waiting for the ambulance, and that pulled me through everything that was to come.

The accident was the critical moment of my life. Everything that has happened since is defined as *before the crash* or *after the crash*. It's been like having two completely different lives.

*

In applying make-up, primer is the base of everything. It lies beneath foundation as the first layer, so that the foundation sits on my skin easily.

I equate that process to my struggles. I am a natural optimist. I prefer to be positive about my difficulties rather than be buried beneath them. Primer is the chance to do that every single time I apply make-up. As I've said, it is the base beneath every stroke of eyeliner, every smudge of eyeshadow, every sweep of the mascara wand.

I had always dreamt of 'making it' in the acting or singing world. Before the accident, I was a regular teenage girl, into singing, amateur dramatics, fashion and make-up. I auditioned for the school talent show and musical each year and always got a good part, though never the lead role! That never bothered me; I just loved being on stage and playing a part or singing a good song. I even played an orphan in Fagin's gang in the musical *Oliver!*. Hardly glamorous. Outside school I attended dance lessons, though I'd be the first to admit dancing was never my strong point! I was never going to be a dancer, but I loved it, and I've always thought that's a good enough reason to do something.

A special moment for me was being chosen to sing at Her Majesty's Theatre. While rehearsing for the production of *Seven Brides for Seven Brothers*, our teacher asked us to sing. She walked round the room, listening to each of us. I was amazed when she picked me! I was so happy to be chosen out of all the talented girls in the dance troupe. I remember so clearly the feeling of standing on the stage in London, not being able to see the audience at all because of the blinding lights, and singing that first note. I thought I'd die of fear! I couldn't hear a word I was singing, but I concentrated on belting it out in the hope I wasn't doing too badly. The experience, though terrifying, taught me to face my fears, to make sure I always did the very thing that scared me, and it definitely put 'stars in my eyes'. That evening gave me a huge confidence boost, and I came home dreaming of moving to the capital to make it big!

Lying in the ditch, not knowing if I would survive, not knowing how badly I was injured or the limitations those injuries would place on my life, was the point where my dreams were crushed – or were they?

Unbeknown to me then, I had the seed of perseverance, the inner confidence born of those earlier, carefree days, that taught me that if I believed I could be a success, then I would be a success. We all have a base – the situation we are in through no fault of our own, our individual circumstances that define who we are. But it's what we do with them that matters. It's the emotional resilience we bring to our lives that is what ultimately defines our successes and achievements, regardless of where we are or who we are. You don't need money to be a success: you need guts, and serious amounts of determination – or that's what I was about to discover.

I had no idea how much I was going to have to relearn over

the next months and years. It would almost be like starting from scratch again, like opening the pages of an elementary textbook of my life. Was I up to it? Can someone really have the courage to begin again? Would I be brave enough?

3

Foundation

Smoothing Over Difficulties

'Gratitude is important, especially in the darkest times.
There is always something to feel grateful for, no
matter how bad things feel.'

My last day as a normal teenager was one of anticipation and excitement. It was a Friday, a school day, but it was also the day of a house party being thrown in the area. Everyone was invited. The guy's parents were away (I didn't know him personally as he went to a different school), and so he'd decided to have a party.

My best friend Cara and I had talked about it for weeks. We were determined to go, and had planned the day like a military operation!

The night before I'd packed my bag with 'going out' clothes: a pair of cool jeans, black high heels and a trendy halter-neck top. I'd also thrown in my straighteners (I never went anywhere without them!) and my bulging make-up bag. We both wanted to look our absolute best, as there would be a lot of older teens there, and so we'd decided to glam it up.

The day was spent waiting for the final bell to ring at the end of the afternoon, so I can't remember much about lessons or what we did that day. Finally it sounded, and I grabbed the bag and my satchel and raced down the corridors to find my friend.

Once out of the clatter of the school, spilling out students in noisy herds, we linked arms and walked back to Cara's house, chattering about who might be at the party and what we were both going to wear. At Cara's we escaped up to her room and put on a CD compilation, mouthing the words to the songs into a hairbrush microphone and messing about as we got ready.

'Busted – my favourite!' Cara grabbed the brush and pretended to sing the track, 'Teenage Kicks', a cover of an original Undertones record.

'Yay, I love that song,' I agreed as I pulled off my uniform and started to dress in my tight jeans and stripy black and white halter-neck top. I had no shame about getting undressed in front of Cara; even though we'd only been mates since the start of Year Ten, when she moved to King's Lynn from Cumbria. We'd quickly become close and now had no secrets from each other.

Then 'Summer of '69' by Bryan Adams came on, and I reached for the hairbrush and did my own version, delighting in being able to sing as I knew all the lyrics. I loved that song!

'You really love singing, Jordan . . .' sighed Cara. She was pulling on her jeans, her dark brown hair swinging as she moved.

'Yeah, I do! You don't even have to be able to sing to actually do it. If you enjoy it, just go for it,' I replied, holding my mirror with one hand and stroking the mascara wand across the eyelashes of my left eye.

'Oh, I love your lippy,' Cara said, rummaging through my make-up bag, 'and your foundation – that's new, isn't it? Oh, can I borrow some?'

I threw the bottle of skin-coloured liquid over to my friend. When it came to beauty and fashion, I was always buying the newest products, so it wasn't unusual for friends to borrow my stuff. I took it as a compliment.

I pushed my heels onto my feet, tightening the straps and wiggling my toes. I pulled back to admire them. They were new. I'd bought them only a couple of weeks before on one of our shopping days together, and was looking forward to wearing them out for the first time. Then I plugged in my straighteners. While they warmed up, I finished applying my make-up. In those days I used lots of purple eyeshadow and had glossy pink lips – looking back, I looked terrible, but at the time I thought I looked the bee's knees!

'Hey, do you reckon Mark will be there? He definitely fancies you!' Cara sniggered, raising an eyebrow in my direction.

I glanced back at her. 'He likes you, and you know it! You're not going to abandon me for a boy, are you?' I half-joked. I knew Cara had her eye on a couple of guys from our year at school who would be there tonight. We both burst into fits of giggles.

'Course I would, if the chance came!' laughed Cara. 'Now come on, let's get going. Have you got the drinks?'

I nodded. We had got hold of some Lambrini – woo-hoo! We never drank much, but there was no way we were going to turn up to an older boy's party with no booze – that would have been social suicide! We were also total lightweights when it came to alcohol; we prided ourselves on how rubbish we were at drinking.

We tottered along the road, a couple of boy mates joining us en route, as they lived nearby.

Arriving in the right street, we were greeted by a large house with well-kept grounds.

'Nice,' said Cara, and nudged me. We both giggled again and knocked on the door. Someone we didn't recognise opened it. He already looked a bit the worse for wear. The party was heaving. We inched our way through the corridor, found the kitchen, where we deposited our drinks, and made for the back garden. The noise from the stereo was blasting so loudly we couldn't hear ourselves speak inside.

Outside there were groups of boys and girls, none of

whom we knew, so we chatted between ourselves.

'Look at me, I can fly!' Towards midnight, a boy who must have been seventeen at most was standing at one of the large bedroom windows. We looked up, thinking it was a joke, and then suddenly he jumped out, rolling into the bushes beneath, staggering back up onto his feet, laughing, being patted on the back by another boy who was clearly very drunk and also quite loud. Then there was another boy, this time standing with his back to the window, looking like he might crash-land as well.

A boy next to us started being sick, so I looked after him for a while, holding his hair back as he puked up and telling him he'd be OK. The whole thing was like the kind of party we saw on American films and TV programmes. They even had the big red plastic cups often seen in those kinds of movies.

'I think it's time to go,' I said to Cara, and she gestured her agreement, nodding her head.

By this time it was late, and I was tired after the week at school, so we reluctantly left. The party felt like it was getting out of control, and we later heard that the police had been called by neighbours. We walked home with some difficulty in our heels across a field, so our boy mates gave us piggybacks and we sang and laughed all the way home. It had been a fun night.

I stayed at Cara's, and the next morning I decided to go into town. I had some photographs I wanted to develop. I remember standing in Boots getting impatient at the size of the queue, not knowing that hours later I'd get the kind of perspective that you hope only comes once in a lifetime. I'd definitely never again become impatient at something as trivial as a queue for photos!

Munching on a custard cream, I headed home, saying 'hi' to Eden on my return and giving her a cuddle even though she was ill with chickenpox. I messaged a few friends on MSN, went to my room to check my make-up and came back down to make beans on toast.

My friend Sarah and I had arranged to meet up, and we decided to walk to the supermarket.

As I left the house, the strangest thing happened.

'Jordan, Jordan, don't go, me not want you to go.' It was Eden, flushed with fever as she toddled after me, trailing her comfort blanket.

'You go on, Jordan, I'll take Eden,' she said, waving to me.

I smiled and blew a kiss to my little sister, then turned to go. But what if I hadn't? What if I'd picked Eden up and settled her down with Mum? Would my destiny have changed? Would Sarah and I have missed bumping into Tim and Jamie? Mum later told me that Eden ran to the door as I shut it.

It is pointless wishing that things could have been different, and yet that moment crystallised into something portentous, as if Eden somehow knew instinctively that she had to stop me. I often wonder how things might have been if I'd heeded her warning. Sometimes life comes down to split-second decisions, and all we can ever do is live entirely in the moment, trusting that the right thing is happening. I didn't stop for Eden. I didn't carry her back in, and so we did meet the boys. The rest, as they say, is history.

The accident became the foundation of my life. Its legacy is in the form of my injuries, and also in the form of the lessons it has taught me, which are now the basis of everything.

When I apply foundation on top of the primer, I use it to smooth over my skin, making it even in colour and tone. It lies on the primer, making my skin appear flawless and making me look healthier. The primer also makes my foundation last longer on the skin.

It is the starting point for all the contouring, sculpting and defining work that comes with the use of highlighter, blush and bronzer, and creates a canvas just like an artist's to work upon. My injury is also that base, that canvas. It is the foundation on which my life has been rebuilt. Everything now comes from that: my need for carers, my daily limitations, but also the greatest lessons on living life to the full that I have been taught. It has given me so much, and I hope to show that to you through this book. Even the most horrendous, traumatic experience can be a gift if we look hard enough. At the very least, experiencing paralysis has given me empathy for others that I would never have had, an understanding of how difficult even the simplest things can be, and a boundless source of gratitude for the help, support and love I am shown daily.

The most important thing it has taught me is that gratitude. I could look back at that teenage girl having fun on the night of the party and be crushed at the thought that I'd lost her forever in the crash. But I choose not to do that. I choose to look at it differently, as I hope you'll see.

My love of make-up was born as a young girl when I used to beg Mum to let me borrow her powder or lipstick. Like the foundations needed by a building, my passion for beauty became my substructure, creating a framework for my recovery on *my* terms. Make-up wasn't the only passion I had, but it did give me something precious later on, a renewed sense of control. It is one of the few things that I have been able to do by myself, and that's why it became so significant in my fight to reclaim myself and to give me some kind of independence in my life. It was always a source of joy and part of my identity, as well as my love for fashion and performing.

At the age of thirteen I had decided to become a 'goth', for a short while wearing smoky black eyes, black nail varnish and black clothes! *So* not me!

Later, at the age of fourteen, Mum took me to Selfridges for my birthday treat. My auntie Jackie had arranged a makeover for me at the Stila counter, where the beauty assistant gave me my bold, beautiful purple eyeshadow. It was the magic that kick-started my devotion. I wore that purple shade every day for months!

What I'm trying to say is that I loved the freedom make-up gave me, and definitely still gives me, to choose who I can be each day. It is a daily act of creation and reinvention, and something I am so happy to be able to do today, though it took hours of painstaking practice.

Can you look at your own life and see the silver linings? Can you find things to be grateful for? If you can, enlarge them, hold them tightly, give thanks for them, because those are the things that will carry you through your life, however troubled or difficult it might be.

So that day I carried on walking. Sarah skipped up beside me from her street nearby. I was wearing a pair of jeans, a pair of green crochet flats I really liked and my favourite pinstriped blazer I'd bought from Debenhams in the sale. It was my all-time favourite jacket.

Then the car drew up.

'Jordan has sustained tetraplegia that is motor- and sensory-complete at the C6 level. She may need to lie on her back for the rest of her life.'

The surgeon, who was wearing his green surgery gown and a hairnet, looked at Mum, then signalled to a nearby nurse that he was leaving the ward.

I couldn't see Mum's face, as I wasn't part of this conversation, but I could imagine her shock, disbelief and anger because those emotions were mine too when I found out, though I was hazy with morphine.

The official description of the spinal injury given on my hospital notes was this: *Jordan sustained a burst fracture of C6 and bilateral lamina fractures of C6. Jordan has a fracture of the body of C7 and unilateral fracture of the lamina of C7 on the right. She has a fracture on the C5 lamina on the right. There was disruption posteriorly of the ligaments between C6 and C7.*

The notes went on to say that tetraplegia was complete at the C6 level – that was the spinal cord damage. The terms tetraplegia and quadriplegia are interchangeable. People often ask me what the difference is between a quadriplegic and a tetraplegic, as both terms are used to refer to my condition. Well, they're both the same. They refer to any spinal cord injury within the cervical sections of C1 and C8. As you know, my injury was at the C6 level. So that's why both names are used to describe me. I guess quadriplegic is better known, which is why I mostly use it, but it doesn't matter either way.

It seems unbelievable, even now, to realise how complete the devastation to my body was. I would never walk again. I might never sit up again. And to make matters worse, my body had swollen, blown up like a balloon as a reaction to the trauma of the accident and injury.

I had been rushed to King's Lynn Hospital in a blue-light dash with sirens blaring, weaving in and out of consciousness. I don't remember the gentle hands of the paramedics working to free me from that car, though they took several hours to complete the delicate procedure. I don't remember being laid on a stretcher, or being inched into the emergency vehicle, either. There were just flashes of images: seeing the roof of the ambulance, the blurry face of a male paramedic. Mum's face swam in and out of the gloom. She was nearby but unable to stroke my face, touch my hand. I guess any movement could've killed me.

'Jordan, sugar, you're going to be fine, I know this is all going to be OK.' Mum smiled, her lovely blue eyes hovering over me, her warm floral scent engulfing me. She has always looked a lot younger than her years. She was only thirty-three when the crash happened.

'My blazer, where's my blazer, Mum?' Puzzled, my thoughts centred on my best jacket, rather than on whether I was alive or injured!

'Don't worry about it – we'll get you a new one as soon as you're better,' Mum soothed.

Woozy now with shock and with the pain relief I had been given, I let myself drift back into dreaming. We must have arrived at the hospital, and my trolley was wheeled off and into the bowels of the building, though I have no recollection of it. Then there were harsh lights, urgent voices, the touch of a nurse, the sound of a machine clunking over my head, which I later realised had been an MRI scanner. I had my clothes cut off. My Glasgow Coma Scale was registered as 15 out of 15 upon arrival, which meant I was conscious, though I don't remember much at all.

Wheeled to intensive care, my bed was placed next to the

nurses' station, which I realise now meant my condition was life-threatening. Then there was the pain again: an intense throbbing at the back of my neck, complete agony.

'My neck, Mum, my neck is killing me,' I wailed.

'Shhhh, darling, we're doing everything we can. Hold in there, lovely.' Mum's face looked white as she leant over me. 'The doctor's here, let's see what he says.'

Only recently, Mum admitted to me that she'd freaked out when the surgeon said I'd have to lie down for the rest of my life, but she'd had to pretend that everything was OK, that one day I would be 'better', though that concept would be stretched to breaking point. I guess she was trying to protect me. We were all entering unknown territory, and I was thankfully oblivious to most of the drama, except the very real pain pounding in my neck.

'I can't feel my feet, Mum, why can't I feel my feet?' I kept asking, though the doctor had said what was happening. The reality didn't register through the shock. The path ahead was going to be long, to coming to terms with those few simple words that I would find out later: 'You are a tetraplegic.'

I learned that the doctor had taken my mum aside to tell her the worst of it. 'Jordan has broken her neck,' the surgeon told her.

'But will it get better?' Mum said.

'Necks don't get better,' he said, his voice softening, knowing he was delivering a shocking blow, 'they don't mend by themselves.' He turned and walked away, his footsteps echoing on the clean floor of the ward.

There was silence then. Mum was lost for words. She came back in to face me and her eyes glistened with unshed tears.

'It's going to be all right, I don't care what the doctors say. It's all going to be OK.'

I had been shielded from the full extent of my condition to prevent further distress, but my mum had to bear the weight of it all. Mum managed a smile, but I know it must have cost her terrible emotional pain to try to bolster me up. The sight of me in that bed, surrounded by bleeping machines, drips and not being able to move, must have been terrifying.

As well as breaking my neck, I had a large laceration on the left side of my forehead, from my temple to my eyebrow. Glass was embedded in my skin, and it wasn't until days later, at a different hospital, that all of it was removed. Fragments of bone from my neck had damaged my spinal column, which was what had resulted in the loss of feeling in my body below my chest.

'Jordan, darling, we're going to have to shave your hair off. As the surgeon said, we need to make sure you have no movement at all around your head and neck.

'We're going to fit a metal halo. It isn't the prettiest of things but it'll protect you, and I'm sorry, but we have to do it.'

I blinked up at the nurse, who had a friendly face and brown hair. Everything felt like an out-of-body experience – things were being done to me without me fully processing what was going on. Didn't she realise that my hair was my pride and joy?

'But I've been growing it for months!' I burst into tears. Losing my hair seemed like a disaster. It's amazing how small things like that take on enormous significance at moments of crisis. Somehow, losing my hair seemed to produce a worse reaction in me than the pain I was in, although I guess I hadn't considered the long-term consequences of my injuries at that point.

'Sorry, darling, it's important. It's all got to go.' The nurse bustled around me. I wanted to shout at her to stop, to go away!

At this point, Mum stepped in. Probably as a reaction to how powerless we all felt, she decided to stop them shaving the whole lot off.

'Why can't you just shave off the areas where the halo will be fitted? Jordan's been through enough already. Losing her hair is like losing herself. I won't let you.' Mum was fierce when she was angry, like a tiger protecting her cub.

The nurses glanced at each other. The one who seemed to be more senior agreed to speak to my surgeon and they both disappeared off to see what could be done. I was amazed when they returned, smiling. Inside I cheered at this small victory as they capitulated, shaving off the hair behind my ears, holding me very gently as they did it. This produced yet more pain as my hair was clogged with my blood (when I was admitted they thought I was a redhead, not a blonde), and highlighted by the shards of glass from the shattered windscreen. As they worked, the glass dug into my skull and I cried out.

The nurses shushed me, saying how brave I was, but I was gutted at losing even those patches of hair. Despite this, when they finished I joked: 'I'm definitely billing you for my hair extensions,' and they both laughed.

Later that day I was taken to surgery and the halo was attached. Six titanium screws were drilled into my skull and the metal ring fitted, screwed into my skull bone to keep my head secure. Then bags of sand were attached as weights. I didn't know it, but everything hung on my lying immobile. My life was in the balance, and my only hope seemed to be a specialist spinal injury ward in Sheffield.

The process of smoothing out difficulties was under way. Now all I had to do was wait for a bed to become free in Sheffield, and hope against hope that something could be done to give me back the life and liberty I lost that day. This was only the beginning of a journey that took me to the very limits of what a human being can endure, yet one which saw me emerging stronger and brighter, like a butterfly from its pupa.

4

Contouring

Shaping the Future

'There is always hope – you just have to believe things will get
better and they will.'

'We're ready for you, darling.' One of the nurses was standing at my bedside. I can't remember what she looked like;
the faces all seemed to merge into one.

'There's a bed free for you in the spinal unit in Sheffield.
It's time to say goodbye to us.'

I looked up at the nurse's friendly face and felt a rush
of hope. Thank God, thank God. Things could be going
right for me. If there was any treatment for my condition,
it would be there. Hope and excitement collided. At last,
something could be done for me.

I beamed back at the nurse, despite the fact that my neck
was still agony.

'Thank you so much for everything, but you know what? I can't wait to leave!'

I'd been at King's Lynn Hospital for five days. Five days spent looking upward, seeing the tops of heads, the stains on the ceiling and little else, all the while waiting to be moved to the Princess Royal Spinal Injuries Centre in Sheffield. All our hopes were fixed on this move. I'd seen doctors and nurses huddled round a medical textbook close to my bed, glancing over at me and talking in whispers. Though everyone was very nice, they seemed to have no idea what to do with me other than keep me alive and stock-still. We knew that where I was going was a specialist hospital, so it seemed that any chance of recovery would be centred around the care I'd receive there.

The five days had felt like five weeks. With nothing to look at except that grubby ceiling, I felt I could go mad with boredom. I was in constant pain, and that made it more difficult mentally to keep cheerful, but despite that, I'd remained upbeat.

I felt sure the answer was in Sheffield, so really it felt more like a waiting game for me.

Mum was incredible. She stayed by my side twenty-four hours a day, sleeping in the plastic hospital chair next to me at night as I lay awake. I couldn't listen to music as they couldn't put headphones on me because of the halo, so I was left to my thoughts.

I can't honestly say how I got through those first days. I

was in massive shock. I was also learning what I *couldn't* feel.

It was so strange, feeling nothing beyond my neck, no sensation at all. The boundaries, the perimeters of my body were lost to me. I could not feel the white cotton sheets against my legs. I couldn't feel the soft breeze on my arms from the open window. I couldn't feel the tight socks the nurses made me wear to prevent blood clots due to my immobility, or an itch anywhere beyond my head.

Just as I was noticing the void of physical sensation, I noticed how my thoughts looped round and round, focusing on those few precious moments before I got into the car. To say they were regrets would be an understatement. The 'what ifs' became a form of mental torture and I cried a lot, though mostly at night when Mum had dozed off, when the insurmountable reality of my situation lay, devastatingly, in full view.

Then the day came when a bed became free for me. Suddenly it was all action, and it felt rather exciting. At least something was happening, at last. Mum hastily packed up my bags.

'Time to go, sugar,' was all she said. 'I can't come with you in the helicopter, I'm afraid; there isn't room.'

'Mum, no, I want you there!' I replied, feeling panicky at the thought of undertaking the journey alone.

'You'll be fine – you'll have a doctor with you, and it won't take long. I'm going to jump in the car now and hopefully get there before you,' she said.

'Drive carefully, Mum,' I replied, and we both looked at each other with a kind of grim recognition. We had one of us in a state because of an accident; we didn't need another.

'I told you I wanted to end up in a city,' I added, a lump forming in my throat. 'It's just not in the way I expected.'

If Mum caught on to my mood, she waved it away as she blew me a kiss. 'I'll get going, as I want to be there in good time for your arrival. Promise me you'll be brave and let them take you. They're all doing their best for you.'

I know Mum was trying to soothe me but I felt like a baby all of a sudden, and had an urge to burst into childish tears at the thought of travelling without her.

'I'll be fine, Mum, don't worry. See you in Sheffield.' I grinned, fighting back tears.

Mum left and a couple of hours later, I was wheeled off to the helipad with my halo attached and the bags of sand that weighted the contraption down hanging off the head end of my bed. Goodness knows how the crew got me into the ambulance. I had my eyes squeezed shut as we neared the sound of the rotating blades. The day was warm. It felt strange being outside for those brief minutes as I was hoisted inside the waiting helicopter. Part of me was thrilled to be on my way. It marked the next stage in whatever recovery I was able to have.

It felt like things were moving forward. Even so, I was terrified of the journey, scared my neck would move or we would crash.

As the blades slashed through the air, the rumble of the engine roared yet I could do nothing to protect my ears. Obviously I couldn't wear ear defenders. The sound was deafening. The helicopter lifted into the sky with jerky movements and I felt like screaming in terror.

Time stretched on; the flight never seemed to end. I felt sick. I wanted desperately for it to stop. The feeling of being utterly helpless was overwhelming.

Then we landed. The rest was a bustle of paramedics and nurses as I was taken out and wheeled into the new hospital. Mum was already there to meet me. I had dreamt of gleaming wards with ultra-modern, twenty-first-century equipment. Imagine my disappointment when I saw the same kind of familiar brown-stained ceilings, shabby curtains round beds and blinking machines. It didn't appear to be any different from King's Lynn!

'There you go, luvvie,' said one of the porters in a distinctive Northern accent as we entered a small shared room off Osbourne 1 Ward.

'You'll be all right in here, ye just give the nurses a shout if ye need anythin', eh?' he added, before walking off whistling an out-of-tune chart hit, leaving a faint trace of cigarette smoke.

For a moment I felt disorientated. My recovery was taking shape. I had arrived at the specialist unit where my chances would be better than if I'd stayed in my local hospital, yet I felt the first twinges of fear. What if there was nothing they could do for me, and that doctor was right? What if I was going to have to get used to lying on my back forever? I hadn't allowed myself to think those thoughts; I'd concentrated on the hope I felt about coming here, staying positive about my future, because if anyone could help me, this team could. It was only on arrival that I allowed myself to consider the possibility that things may not be as hopeful as I'd wanted them to be. That disappointment felt crushing, yet I couldn't let myself fall into negative thinking.

I had no idea yet what my real prognosis might be. It was a battle to fight off those unhelpful thoughts, but I knew I had to do it. I could feel I was hovering on the edge of an abyss, a place where dark feelings swirled inside me, and so I fought with all my strength of mind to remain on the side of the light. After all, there is always hope. There has to be. With every breath I stayed alive, and that was surely a miracle already.

Mum came with me to my shared room. I don't think I have ever been more pleased to have her with me.

'How was it? Was the flight OK?' she asked, her eyes studying my face. She could tell I was struggling.

I just groaned in response.

'Let me go and get us both a cuppa. I've brought some straws so you can sip a tea. We're going to get through this, d'you hear me, Jordan? We will, I promise you.'

I smiled at that, though the sight of the hospital and my dashed expectations had made me feel strangely heartbroken.

Mum popped to the hospital café. Again I was left staring up into space as nurses moved around me, settling me in, saying soothing things, chattering brightly to me. They were very kind, and the memories of those days always fill me with gratitude at the care I was given.

Yet it amazed me that there was nothing to look at posted up there on the off-white, greyish ceiling – no bright, happy pictures, no words to read, nothing. A small TV lay dormant in the corner. When you think that the unit specialised in spinal trauma, which would mean a lot of people spending the same hours staring up, unable to move their heads, it is remarkable that there was hardly anything to relieve the boredom. Each second ticked by so slowly.

As I stared, the room was suddenly cast into light. Across the ceiling was a creamy, yellowy shaft of summer sunshine. The dust motes seemed to dance in its wake. Suddenly the pain in my neck seemed to recede as I stared at it, revelling in its beauty and the sheer unadulterated hope it gave me. Something about that moment spoke to me in a profound way. There *was* hope. I must *never* give up. I had everything to fight for, to live for.

With a cracked voice, I opened my mouth and very quietly began to sing. It sounded more like a whisper, as I was having difficulty breathing. Searching in my mind for the words, I remembered the song from *Seven Brides for Seven Brothers* I'd sung as a soloist:

I could run but the feeling is there
No place anywhere can hide me
I'm in love and I don't have a chance
I can't stop that voice inside me
Love never goes away, it plays on like a song
Oh, love never goes away, he holds me and I know where I
  belong.

The lyrics felt meaningful to me. I couldn't run from my imprisonment, inside the metal cage that was, in effect, keeping me alive. I couldn't hide from my predicament. The words felt like another mantra; they soothed me and kept me calm while I waited for Mum to come back. I repeated them over and over, barely noticing when Mum pulled the curtain open gently, her face soft.

'Oh, Jordan, you're singing again. Sorry, don't let me interrupt; it was just such a joy to hear you. If you're singing then I know that my beautiful girl is still in there, underneath it all.' Mum put down the paper cups that held our cups of tea and felt for my hand, gently holding my twisted fingers, hands that would never work again.

'Do you remember, I was so nervous about singing that in front of an audience. I really messed up the rehearsal and the teacher got cross with me. I was so upset!'

It seemed amazing to me now to get upset about something so trivial. I doubt I'd ever do that again.

'You were so bloody brave, Jordan, getting up on that

stage. My heart was in my mouth. I think I was more nervous than you, thinking you'd be too scared to get the words out, but you really went for it.' Mum laughed, remembering that evening at Her Majesty's Theatre in London.

'Yeah, and the feeling at the end was amazing, everyone clapping, knowing I must have done all right, but I hadn't been able to hear myself at all. It was just the best feeling.' I grinned over at Mum. 'That's one thing the crash hasn't taken off me . . .'

At that point another doctor appeared at my bedside, a younger consultant with dark hair, but they all get muddled up in my memory. He asked to speak to my mum and they moved away from my bed. I wasn't ever told things directly at this point, because I was only fifteen.

'I've got good news for you. We've looked at Jordan's MRI scans and we think we can perform an operation to rebuild her neck.'

'That's amazing news. How soon can you do it? What does it mean for her and her condition?' Mum asked.

'We won't know until we've been in and seen the extent of the damage. But it is possible that we can use bone from other parts of Jordan's body to strengthen her neck. There are risks, and we'll talk you through those nearer the time. But we can safely say that we can set a date in the next couple of weeks.' He finished.

'It could be weeks?' Mum echoed. Suddenly that seemed very far away. But, and it was a huge 'but', there was an operation. This was fantastic news. Imagine our relief!

Mum came back over and grinned at me. Her eyes were filled with tears.

'Don't start crying, Mum, or I'll start too, and I don't think I'll be able to stop!'

In the meantime, the shape of my day was formed, the contours of my existence as we waited for the surgery.

Every two hours my body was rolled from side to side to prevent bedsores, which meant even the little sleep I managed was disturbed. When they rolled me to the left I saw a grey drug locker, and when they rolled me to the right I saw the armchair Mum sat in. That was the size of my world. Every morning I would be washed carefully in bed, then Mum would try and help me eat some toast or porridge for breakfast. The rest of the day would be punctuated by nurses or doctors appearing, running tests, and being taken for scans. The hours blurred together, formless, as we waited with what felt like baited breath for the operation that could change everything.

I didn't know it at the time but the surgeon had taken Mum aside and told her I may not survive it, and that if I did, there was a risk the procedure could make my injury worse, and that because they were operating on my neck my vocal cords could be severed. That would mean no talking and no singing ever again. I don't know how Mum kept up her cheery smile and constant chatter knowing that, but she did. She was amazing.

I'm so lucky to have had her by my side. Growing up, Mum and I were always very close. She had me at the age of eighteen, and we became a tight little family unit. We were a one-parent household; I never knew my dad, and it never bothered me.

Mum and I lived with her mum, Nanno Margaret, for the first couple of years after I was born. Then we moved to a tiny flat with a garden, and so all my memories of growing up were with Mum, playing in our small outside space, or going over to Grandad John's house. John was my mum's dad, and he was like a father figure to me. I never felt deprived, not having my real father around, although, weirdly, I did do a drawing at the age of four which I remember really well. I drew a picture of me, Mum, our cat, my dad and a pretend sister. I made up our 'family' because everyone else we knew had one like that. I did it to try and fit in, I guess, which was strange because I felt happy as a child, and very content with it just being me and Mum.

Nanno Margaret and Grandad John had separated way before I was even around, and they lived in different places. Mum always used to tell me I was extra lucky because I had more grandparents' homes to visit!

Waiting for the op meant I had lots of time to go over old memories, and I kept myself as upbeat as possible by remembering how, as a little girl, Grandad John would spoil me. We went over there every other Saturday afternoon. I would help Grandad water his plants, as he was very green-fingered, and try and tend to his tortoise, who seemed to be in permanent hibernation! Every time I went over there, he'd hold out both his hands, folded into fists, and ask me to choose one. I'd always pick both because I knew he'd always have a small present in each – a sweetie or a little toy. It was our 'thing', and I adored him for it. Then Grandad John would read out the names of the racehorses for me to pick one for him to back. Every time I went for the most 'girly'-sounding one, or a rider wearing a pink-coloured jersey! Poor Grandad must've had a chuckle when he went to the bookies' and told them why I'd picked his 'gee-gee', as he called the horse.

My one consolation through all this was that Grandad was too ill with Parkinson's disease to fully understand what had happened to me. He had been living in a care home for several years, and I knew he would be completely oblivious, which actually was a blessing. He had started losing his memory years ago, and even before the crash he struggled to remember things about me. I didn't mind. I was just happy that he was well cared for. He was so special to me; to all of us.

My memories gave me hope. They showed me that it is the little things in life, the love we receive, the small moments of joy, that make life worth living. They proved that it isn't how rich or how perfect we are that makes us happy; it is the people in our lives who love us, and who we love, that is the core of true contentment. Yet despite this, everything was pinned on this op.

One day, something happened: Mum spotted movement in my foot.

'Jordan, did you do that?' She stood up as she spoke, looking over at me eagerly.

'Yes, I think so,' I replied. 'I can't be sure, but yes, it definitely moved, Mum.'

We looked at each other, hope written across our faces. What rookies we were. We didn't have any understanding, really, of spinal injury, even then.

Mum ran over to a male nurse standing at the nurses' station.

'Jordan's foot moved, it definitely moved. What does it mean?' she panted with excitement.

Without moving his head, or stopping the note he was writing, he said one word, 'Spasm,' crushing Mum in the process. I could have wept for her. She stood for a moment. I guess she was composing herself before she came back to me, this time her smile looked forced.

'It's probably a spasm, darling. We'll know more after the operation.' I didn't ask any more. I was devastated. We dropped the subject and turned the television on, both lost in our thoughts.

The day of the op arrived. The procedure would take six hours, repairing the broken bones in my neck by grafting bone from my hip. I had fractured the C6 vertebra in my neck, which had damaged my spinal column.

'So, let me get this right,' I said to my surgeon, 'if the operation is successful, then you'll be able to take off the metal halo?'

'Yes, that's correct,' he replied. 'Though there are risks, as we've explained to your mother.'

I ignored that part of the conversation.

'So I'll be able to sit upright again?' I added, and he nodded back at me. I looked around at the hundreds of cards from well-wishers, the pink fluffy soft toys and cushions people had sent in for me to decorate my room with.

'I might be able to sit again,' I echoed, starting to smile. 'Let's do it – forget the risks, I'm ready,' I finished.

'Your daughter is a fighter, I'll give her that,' the surgeon said to Mum, and she laughed back, 'Don't I know it, and thank God she is!'

On the morning of the op I was not allowed food or water. Another MRI scan was done, but that's when things rolled to a halt.

'What's going on?' I asked a nearby nurse. 'Why haven't they taken me down for surgery? I've been waiting all day.' It was almost 4 p.m., and the day had stretched out in a sea of endless waiting.

'I'll check what's happening, though it looks like it won't be today, my dear,' was all she said, and a consultant came back to us within minutes, confirming it.

'Your procedure has been postponed,' he said. 'The MRI scan we did has revealed that you've cracked your C5 and C7 vertebrae, and it's more tricky than we thought. It's going to be a much more complex operation than we previously realised. I'm sorry, there's nothing we can do about it. As soon as we know when it can take place, we'll tell you.'

And that was it. Reeling from the news, I burst into sobs of real despair, the first I'd really allowed myself at Sheffield. I howled like an injured animal. Mum sat beside me, waiting patiently for me to finish, rubbing my hand.

'Come on, lovely, it's just another few days to wait,' Mum crooned, stroking my right hand, sitting close to my bed. 'Look at all the people who are rooting for you. Look at all your cards – that's got to give you hope. And they're still doing the op; they haven't told you they can't do it. It'll be OK, I know it will; just hold in there.'

If I could have squeezed Mum's hand gratefully I would've done. I finished my tears and Mum gently wiped them away with a soggy tissue, showing she'd had a cry herself earlier that day. I said nothing, though. I felt bad that I'd given her more to worry about.

Then, 'I'm fine,' I said. 'I'm totally fine. It was just the shock, but it'll be OK. Don't worry about me, honestly.'

But I wasn't fine. I was in agonising pain from my neck injury. I felt I would never get out of this hospital bed. But Mum was there for me, and as long as I lived and breathed there was always hope.

Five days later, at the end of May, I was wheeled to another, dingier part of the hospital and onto the operating ward. Cannulas were placed into my veins, which of course I couldn't feel, and then a nurse peered over me, telling me to count to ten. The theme tune to my favourite TV programme, *The O.C.*, was playing in the background, which made me happy.

'One, two, three . . . four . . .' and I was out.

Six hours later – though it felt like minutes – the recovery ward came into focus. It was dark and a bit grim. Blinking, it took a split second to realise that I was in agonising pain. My neck was excruciating. I cried out. A nurse came over and I begged her for pain relief.

'I'm sorry, my dear, but we gave you some a couple of hours ago, so you can't have anything else for a few hours.'

'But I'm in pain. It's agony!' I wanted to shout, but even that felt too painful.

'I'm sorry, my dear, there's nothing we can do. Try to rest.'

With that, the nurse disappeared. I could have roared in my distress and confusion. I knew that because I was still only fifteen (though a few months away from being sixteen) I could only have a child's dose of morphine, but this time it wasn't nearly enough.

It felt like I lay there for hours as nurses moved around me, machines beeped and footsteps echoed on the floors.

I had no power over my body. I could not move an inch. I

was in terrible pain that was seemingly endless, but I realised again what I *could* do. I could sing to myself in my head.

I don't know why, but I returned to the song I sang to keep myself awake during the crash. Perhaps it felt like the same kind of emergency, the same battle to keep my spirit, and perhaps myself, alive. Mum was still waiting for me to come round in a different part of the hospital, so I was alone and I didn't know when they'd let me see her.

I thought of the lyrics that by now had so much significance for me: *You've got the love I need to see me through . . .*

I felt I was singing for my life, my soul, again. It was the only way I could acknowledge that I wasn't beaten, that I could survive, could get through this. I don't know whose or what's 'love' was seeing me through; I just knew the words made sense to me again, and so I kept going with them, burning them into my heart. I didn't hear Mum's footsteps as she approached. I didn't hear her walk to my bedside. My eyes were closed in supplication to my personal search for the strength I needed to *see me through*.

My life had been abruptly, shockingly shaped by forces out of my control. The contours of my life and my body were fundamentally and brutally changed. I'd undergone a surgical redesign and I had survived it. So far, so good.

Being a survivor, I've had the chance to reflect. I often mull over how parts of my life equate to my beauty routines;

how we are prepping, priming, bettering and defining ourselves. In beauty terms, after the primer and foundation are
applied, that's when I start the contouring, using shade and
light to redesign my face. I apply dark shades to places I
want to recede a little, and light shades to places I want to
bring forward, because I don't want my face to look flat. I
like it to have definition, to be the best it can be.

For example, I contour the top of my forehead, adding
bronzer to the edges then highlighting across the middle.
I use bronzer to shape my cheekbones, running the brush
underneath the line of the bone, then using highlighter
along the top. The effects can be almost as good as plastic
surgery, and a hell of a lot cheaper!

The operations, and the trauma of the accident, have
reshaped my life in every possible way. I am defined by what
happened on every level: physically, emotionally and mentally. The surgery started a process of rebuilding, through
restructuring my neck. That was the catalyst for my life to
move forward, albeit slowly.

Contouring is a process of building on what is there
and improving it, making it better. For me it has been an
important process, and one which started in so many ways
as a result of the surgeon's work on my body.

Though I would never be cured, my abilities were being
reshaped, my strengths redesigned, and that's all I needed to
start on the long path of recovery.

5

Complexion

Being True to Myself

'Be the authentic YOU! Always be yourself – don't let anybody, or anything, change you.'

'Jordan is doing really well, she's a real trooper,' the surgeon said. He was stood at the end of my bed. I could see the top of his dark hair but little else. Mum was standing beside me, clutching my right hand. I could feel her shake a little.

'So, was it a success? Will Jordan be able to move again? What is her prognosis?' The questions tumbled out of Mum's mouth.

'It's OK, Mum, let the surgeon speak,' I said softly, even though I was desperate to hear whether my operation had worked. I wanted Mum to know that even if it hadn't, there was no room for despair. We'd be OK, whatever.

'The operation went very well,' the surgeon replied. I

could hear that he was smiling from the tone of his voice.

'We made an incision in the front of Jordan's neck, around her throat and at the back of her neck. This was because the vertebrae were cracked, as we told you. We managed to graft bone from her hip to the damaged area to rebuild it, and we've stabilised the fracture with a series of metal plates and screws.

'As you know, Jordan did not lose her voice, which is always the worry when we have to go in at the front. As you can see, because the neck has been rebuilt we were able to remove the halo and instead put a rigid plastic neck brace to keep Jordan steady while the bone transplant fuses.

'We consider the operation to have been a complete success, though we did have to give Jordan a blood transfusion as she lost a lot of blood.'

'But will she be OK?' Mum interjected.

'It depends what you mean by OK,' the surgeon replied. 'In terms of the procedure, we're very happy with how it went, but we have to wait now for the graft to settle. Then we can start the process of getting Jordan to sit up. But it'll be slow, and we need to go carefully, raising her bed by twenty degrees at a time. Try not to rush.

'It's important Jordan stays positive and is patient. We've done everything we can, for now at least.'

'Thank you, doctor,' was all I managed to reply. Tears pricked my eyes, but I was determined not to let them fall – not in front of Mum, anyway. Mum thanked the surgeon as well. She sat down heavily next to me and exhaled.

'Thank goodness for that. I guess it's just another waiting game now. And we'd better get you eating properly again; you look like a little bird, you've lost so much weight already.'

Mum was right. I'd barely eaten anything in the aftermath of the crash. The shock had robbed me of my appetite, and now I felt sick every time a steaming plate of hospital food was placed in front of me. I was also a vegetarian – had been since I was barely in my teens – and so the choices on the menu were quite limited.

'I know, I'm going out to get you a pizza, then we'll sit and watch a bit of TV while you get on with grafting that neck bone!' I knew that Mum was still reeling, even though the surgeon had given us good news. We were both in a state of shock so absolute that each new piece of information seemed to take ages to absorb properly.

'OK, but then will you tell me when Eden is coming to visit? I can't wait to see her.' I was missing my little sister terribly, and had been devastated that I couldn't be at home for her fourth birthday, which fell ten days after my crash.

Eden was born when I was eleven, and so in some ways I was more like a second mummy to her than a big sister. I would shush her in the evenings and rock her until she fell asleep on me. I would help Mum feed her the mashed veggies and baby food in her high chair as a toddler. She had the biggest blue eyes you've ever seen. In other words, she was a real cutie.

The only thing I wouldn't do was push her buggy, because one day as Mum and I walked along the road past a pub, an elderly man asked if she was mine. I was mortified! After that, I didn't like to touch the buggy in public. Anyway, I adored my little sister, and had missed her badly because she always made me laugh.

Mum had announced that this coming weekend she would go home for the first time. Her partner Darren had visited with Eden every weekend since the accident, but I'd been quite out of it for the first couple of visits.

Now that I had a plastic brace, I think the sight of me was less distressing for my little sister than seeing me in that awful halo.

The day came for Mum to leave.

All of a sudden, I felt small and rather vulnerable again, though I was being cared for brilliantly by the nursing staff. Mum shouted, 'Bye, Jordan, bye, darling, see you soon. I won't be long! You're going to be fine!' as she left the ward, I felt a lump form in my throat. It was the first time I'd been here by myself, and even that wouldn't be for long because my aunt, Mum's sister Jackie, was due in soon to replace Mum at my bedside during the day.

I guess it felt like I was left with just me and my injury, especially in the depths of the night. I felt so shaky about this that the night staff set up a baby monitor so I could call them if I needed someone there! I think it was at this point that I truly realised this had happened to me and me alone.

I know that sounds silly, obvious even, but Mum had been there every waking moment, and every asleep moment too, and so it had felt like it had happened to 'us'. But it hadn't. It was *me* lying there, unable to move, with a brace that dug into my collarbones, with pain in my neck, with the frustration of being unable to move. Just *me*.

Suddenly my world became one of shadows, and long, overnight hours when darkness curled round me, when I felt utterly helpless, like a baby. Of course, I turned to singing to soothe me, choosing songs from musicals, anything that expressed the kind of yearning for freedom that the nights left me with.

Through expressing myself with those songs, I stayed in touch with my inner voice, my true character, the complexion of me and my identity. In the beauty world, our complexion is an expression of the overall character of our skin; its hue, its colouring, its texture and pigmentation. Those songs were my expression of the depth and texture of my soul during those long nights.

It's impossible to achieve a great complexion just through using make-up and products, as so many things like diet, lifestyle and protection are at the root of your skin and its appearance.

The make-up I apply goes on top of the groundwork of a decent skincare routine: cleansing, toning and moisturising each night. Then I know which products suit my skin type and which don't. It's a complex mix, and it involves a degree of reality, assessing your particular skin type and working within that framework.

Looking back, I can see that I was discovering my new reality during those nights alone, though I was far from truly accepting it.

A couple of weeks later, in June 2005, my brace was replaced with a softer version that wasn't so sore to wear. Each small triumph became a marker on my journey back to some kind of 'normality'.

Then a major breakthrough happened.

'Jordan, love, we're going to start sitting you up. The doctors say the bone has had time to fuse, so we can raise your bed by twenty degrees under your head.'

The male nurse, whose face I couldn't see, had taken the control that operated my bed, and it started to shudder into movement very slowly.

'Oh my God, I'm moving up in the world! This is *so* exciting. Wow, I can see the tops of the drip poles! I can see your hair; it's brown. Ha, ha, I'm so happy!'

It sounds crazy, but I really was blown away by this new development. Sitting up even at such a small incline felt like a luxury after weeks of lying flat!

'I can see part of the wall, and the top of the ward door,' I giggled as the bed settled into position, relishing this gigantic move forward in my recovery.

And the best thing about it was that my little sister was

coming up with Darren – she'd be here any minute. I would actually get to see her for the first time since the accident, without my halo or the horrible hard neck brace.

An hour later, the door to my room flew open and Eden ran in ahead of Mum, who was chatting with her partner as they walked in.

'Jordan, you're sitting up! Well, a bit, anyway!' Mum almost shouted in her excitement. 'This is amazing. Sugar, how does it feel? Is it sore?'

'I'm fine, Mum, honestly. I'm so happy to see Eden. Hey, li'l sis, come here and let me see you.'

Eden was a chirpy, bright little girl, and would be starting school that year. When she saw me she stopped and stood still for a moment, unsure how to approach me. Every time she saw me she was a little taken aback at first, but she soon adapted, as young children do. My heart bled for her, though. She looked so confused to see me lying there, when by rights I should've been at home, playing dolls with her or chasing her round the garden.

I had so many happy memories of playing with Eden. The best was probably when she was two years old, just a toddler. I was thirteen, and had filled the paddling pool with water that summer and was introducing the concept of swishing her feet in it. It was lovely seeing her face light up when she began splashing, gurgling with happiness at that simple activity.

Seeing her now, I was bursting with pride. For her sake I

had to become a big sister again, I had to get 'better', whatever that meant, and create a new life for myself, however much I was limited. I had to show her that there is always a brighter future if you dare to wish for it, and that by staying true to myself, the authentic 'Jordan Bone', I could carve out some way of living, as long as I believed in myself and my abilities hard enough. I owed it to her, and to all of my family, who showed me every day how much they loved me. In some ways I was so blessed, and I could see that, despite my situation.

'Come here, gorgeous girl, and show me that new doll of yours. She's a beauty. How many Barbies have you got now? Probably even more than me!'

Everyone laughed at that. My nickname given by the nurses was 'Barbie', as I was surrounded by everything pink: cards, pillows, cushions and throws. I was pink-obsessed as a teenager! Barbie had been my favourite toy as well, so the name really did fit me.

That day was really special, though it did feel a little strange at first, lying even at such a small incline. I felt quite dizzy, and when the nurse came to buzz my bed back down to its flat position, I was secretly relieved. My neck muscles had become so weak they couldn't support my head, so I knew it was something I'd have to build up gradually; two hours upright (-ish!) per day for now, or so the nurse had said.

However, it felt momentous. The shadows receded, for

now, and I felt a new surge of optimism. The next day I was lying elevated again in bed, sucking a boiled sweet. The nurses came in to shift my bed back down while Mum played 'aeroplanes' with Eden, holding her in her arms and swinging her round while making engine noises! I was laughing so much I accidentally swallowed the sweet whole just as my body was lying flat. I started choking, but no one realised – they thought it was part of the fun!

The nurses ran back in, realising by now that I wasn't faking. My face had gone grey, and they performed assisted coughing, pressing me in between my ribs to force me to splutter the sweet back up.

Afterwards we laughed so much, but at the time it was quite frightening. It is one of my most enduring memories of my hospital days!

Things moved on. I started having regular physiotherapy to move my legs and keep the circulation going. This involved the physio stretching my legs up and down, bending them and massaging various points where the muscles had wasted. My days and nights were punctuated by being rolled to each side, and the wound on the back of my neck from the surgery was taking its time healing and felt very sore. I was very lucky not to get MRSA, as it was an open wound and made me vulnerable to catching hospital bugs.

I still had a lot of time to myself, even with Mum and the nurses coming and going. I couldn't help but muse over

some of the challenges I'd faced in the couple of years leading up to the accident, mainly the bullying and rejection I'd
experienced. I don't know why this haunted me now.

Perhaps it was because I had the chance to properly process what had happened, to put it to rest.

Or perhaps it was an opportunity to remember something I'd overcome, a difficult situation that had caused me
pain, but one which I'd faced up to in my own way, and
by doing so could strengthen my coping skills now. Who
knows? Revisiting it felt important.

Being a teenager wasn't the easiest time for me. Is it for
anyone? A group of girls I'd been close to since primary
school decided to turn on me, and since they (previously,
we) were the popular crowd, everyone else followed their
lead. As I anxiously walked through the school canteen I'd
hear whispers of *she's so stuck up* targeted at me.

During bad times, I'd stare at the clock on the wall so I
didn't have to face the nasty girls throwing insults at me. I
probably looked like I was holding my head up high with
pride, but in reality I was just looking ahead to avoid the
glares. Every day I would dread lunchtimes, as I would have
no one to sit with. I felt so alone.

Then one day, after a particularly horrible PE lesson
where I'd been sneered at for the way I ran, I was cornered.

'It's stuck-up Jordan. How are you, Miss Stuck-Up?' sim-
pered one of the five girls that circled round me.

I could feel rather than see the other four hovering at the corner of my vision.

Suddenly the cloakroom at Springwood High seemed to empty. Where moments earlier there had been the noise of girls talking as they got changed, packing up their gym bags to head off for home, as PE had been the last period of the day, there was now no one there at all – except us.

I stepped back instinctively, feeling my hand touch the tiles that lined the wall of the corner which had once been showers, but were now just part of the changing room.

'Hi, girls, what's happening?' I said with enforced calm, though my hackles had risen. I felt sweat prickle under my arms and on my forehead, indicating the instinctive knowledge of a threat posed, subtle yet menacing.

Another girl stepped towards me. This time it was she who spoke, mocking my voice, making it higher than it really was as she copied what I'd said.

'*Hi there, girls,*' she said, adding her own embellishment, '*what's happening, because I'm soooooo cool I don't even know.*'

I gaped back at her. Her face was cocked to the side, watching the effect her behaviour was having on me.

'Is Miss Stuck-Up lost for words?' echoed the ringleader, smiling in a way that made her face look as cold as ice.

'No, I'm not lost for words. I'm just saying hello; there's nothing wrong with that, is there?' I answered, keeping my head high and my arm on my bag as if I expected someone to pounce on it.

These girls used to be my friends, making their treatment of me incredibly puzzling as well as heartbreaking. Now they had cornered me and were treating me like a hounded animal caught by a group of snarling wolves.

I felt like their prey.

The previous term had been my best time at school with these girls. I'd hung out with them all, been part of the gang, swapping jokes and messages on Messenger, texting and meeting at the shops on Saturdays. I was entering teenage life, and it was before my accident, which happened in Year Ten. We were known at the school for being inseparable. We were the popular girls, and it was a great feeling to be in their group. We were the first to be invited to any party or sleepover. Every Saturday we hung out in town, mucking around and chatting about people we knew. I loved every minute.

They weren't known as the school bullies and I'd say, even now, after what they put me through, that they weren't horrible people; they just turned on me, and, I guess, like sheep, everyone else followed.

But I did know that I was now in big trouble, and I couldn't run for it because they had me surrounded.

My mind swirled. My instinct was to burst into unhappy tears, to feel sadness that people I counted as friends were now being so mean to me. But I was stronger than that, though inside I was screaming, feeling that sense of being trapped like a caged animal.

At the end of the holidays, I'd been staying at a friend's with two of the girls when Mum came to pick me up to take me into Cambridge, to stay at my auntie's for a couple of days. When I came back from the trip, they were still really friendly, but I invited them to come to town with me and they said they couldn't. It was no big deal, but when I was in the shopping centre with Mum, I caught sight of them together in Topshop, laughing over something one of them had said. My heart stopped, and I froze.

'Mum, look, it's them. They told me they couldn't come into town,' I said, staring over at where they were standing by a clothes rail, picking out a garment. They couldn't see me but I could see them.

They linked arms and turned to leave the shop, and that's when they saw me. It had always been us three, never just two, out together. Their faces registered shock and a glimpse of guilt. They smiled in a fake way as I walked up and said 'hi'. I don't recall them replying at all; they kind of looked at each other and shrugged, then practically ran out of the shop.

I can't describe how I felt. It was like having my stomach punched. I'd thought we were as close as sisters. In fact, I knew that I was closer to each of them individually than they were to each other, and yet they'd lied to me.

That felt really weird, really horrible.

'They probably just changed their minds and couldn't get hold of you,' replied Mum, trying to make light of it to spare my feelings. She looked at me, and we both looked over at them. I double-checked my phone. No missed calls. No texts or messages.

I looked back over. My former friend with blonde hair was doubled up with laughter. As she giggled I felt the taste of bile in my throat. The bitterness of their betrayal.

I bit my lip.

'Yeah, I'm sure you're right, Mum. Let's go to New Look – I've seen some shoes I like.'

I smiled at Mum, but I could tell she knew how hard I'd taken it.

'I'll treat you,' she said brightly, and we walked off. I found it hard to concentrate for the rest of the weekend. I didn't get the shoes, I didn't have the heart for buying clothes or being treated. I wanted to know why my friends had left me out, and why I felt I was suddenly on the outside. I didn't hear anything from them the next day, and I didn't chase them, either.

It was almost time to start school again, so I decided to leave it until I saw them. Later I did ask them why they'd left me out, but they both got annoyed with me and I never got an answer. I prefer to be direct about things, especially if they are bothering me. It's always best to be honest and open about things before they fester, but I guess they didn't share my feelings.

It wasn't long before I found out that leaving me out of the shopping trip was only the beginning of the bullying that would see me almost friendless in the months ahead.

Now I found myself standing there in the dingy, tiled corner of an old shower area, waiting to see what the girls circled around me would do. I looked at the ringleader, meeting her eyes squarely, determined not to show how afraid I was. I hoped she'd see that what she was doing was wrong. Her actions wounded me the most. She had even written me a letter over that summer saying: 'I hope we stay friends forever.'

'We'll be famous, and not stuck in McDonald's or wear Clownies' (these were the gold necklaces worn by the hard girls who posed a physical threat to anyone who crossed them at school).

How did she go from that, to threatening me in the cloakroom?

I was standing near the old shower by my locker in the corner of the room. I was effectively cut off from the exit. I could feel my heart banging against my chest, but I refused to speak. What were they going to do to me? I thought about yelling for help, but I knew that all the teachers were back in the main building as it was the end of the day. I knew that no one in my class would help, either, even if they heard me. I was stuck, waiting, my panic growing by the second. My mind was crowded with anger and frustration, the echoes of all the nasty comments that had been flung in my direction.

The sneering continued. The ringleader led the mockery, but the others joined in.

'Think you're better than us.'

'Lady Stuck-Up thinks she's better than us. What d'ya say, girls?'

'Yeah, thinks she's better than us . . .'

'Stuck-up cow.'

The voices became distorted. My senses went into over-drive with terror. From nowhere, a feeling of rage bubbled up inside me. I'd had days of being teased, ignored, humiliated and taunted. I'd had enough. I didn't care what I did then; I just wanted to get the hell out of that cloakroom and get home to Mum.

Without thinking, I felt my hand whip up and slap one of them hard on the side of her face. By now there wasn't a ringleader; they were all joining in the taunts with equal force.

Before she had time to react, I bolted.

As I moved I swung my bag to stop anyone grabbing me, but I think they were as shocked as I was.

Nice, sweet Jordan had hit back at last. It was the last thing any of us, including myself, expected. Unsurprisingly, they never ganged up on me like that again, and later on I even became friends again with one of the girls. The episode left me with emotional scars, but it also left me with the knowledge that I didn't change for them; I hadn't become one of the 'sheep' and gone along with their treatment of me. I stayed, authentically, myself.

That knowledge of my essential character – my complexion – had stayed with me. I drew on it in hospital now.

At this point I decided to set the goal of getting strong enough to sit in a wheelchair by 1 July. I don't know why I chose that date. I needed something to focus on. Mum has always said that mentally and emotionally I'm very strong. I guess I've had to be throughout my life. I never knew my dad. We never had much money growing up. I was bullied, yet recovered from that in the only way I knew how, by forging ahead regardless, creating a new life for myself each and every time.

So the task was set. Every day I imagined being strong enough to sit in a chair. Every day I told the nurses it was one less day of lying down.

Above my bedhead the nurses had written a big note: 1 JULY MOBILISE. I counted the days, praying my body would withstand the test. I'd asked Mum to do my hair for me properly as well, to mark the big event of moving into the chair. I was really excited to think that I might even start looking like my true self again. Life felt more hopeful; time seemed to pass more quickly, and I was looking forward to sitting up properly in the way I used to long for days hopping round London on the tube, going shopping and getting free makeovers at the beauty counters.

The challenge had been set. I felt a new sense of purpose. I would move forward with my life and recovery – on my own terms.

6

Concealer

Hiding My Fears

'Never lose sight of your dreams –
they point the way to your happiness.'

'Oh my God, I'm not sitting in *that* . . .' I looked over at
the nurses who had wheeled in the massive, *enormous*, hideous, big black wheelchair that was now sitting next to my
bedside. The women, both in their mid-forties, smiled in an
apologetic kind of way but still stood there, one of them
holding the bars that steered the monstrous great thing.

I appealed to Mum.

'Mum, seriously, I'll look like a freak, like Frankenstein
in that thing! Yeah, that's it, that's what I'm going to call it,
Frankenstein's Chair . . . Really, honestly, Mum, I hate it and
there's absolutely no way I'm getting in it.'

My fury at the sight of the chair I'd been so excited about

masked the bitter disappointment I was experiencing.

I'd been fighting hard to get to this point, getting stronger every day, doing my physio, sitting up despite the pain in my neck, for longer and longer periods. All of it because I was desperate to move on to the next stage of my recovery, the bit where I became mobile again, the bit where I became more *human* again.

Days earlier I'd written a letter to my friend Katie. Even though the note is short, it shows me how much I was looking forward to the next chapter of my life:

To Barbie Katie,
(We called each other Barbie as a term of affection, and we both perhaps not so secretly wanted to look like her!)
  Thanks 4 all of my letters!
  I get in my chair tomoz, yay!

The letter had taken me ages to write. Mum had propped a red felt-tip pen in my hand and helped to guide me as I tried to convey the happiness I felt at getting into my own wheelchair. It is hard to remember now how much I longed for freedom, any kind of freedom, to move around by myself, or even just to get out of that hospital bed! The letter looks like it has been scrawled by a child, but it was a huge achievement at the time, and its simplicity belies the hopes I'd pinned on having a small taste of independence once more.

I don't know what I'd been expecting. Maybe I thought I'd get one of those gleaming, silver, funky wheelchairs the Paralympic athletes use with super-slim wheels and nimble steering.

This chair wasn't like that at all! It looked like something from a freak show. It brought the harsh new reality of my life into sharp focus. In that moment as I lay there, emotion building inside me, I could only ask again, why me? Why had this happened to me?

How did I go from the fifteen-year-old who had made loads of new friends, had a Saturday job in a clothes store and was planning on going travelling with mates after college, to this? How did all my plans, my desires, my dreams arrive at this?

My life had finally turned good in Year Ten, after the pretty grim year of being bullied previously. I'd faced that and made some new friendships, in particular with my friend Cara. I remember when she walked into our classroom for the first time, she said I was the one who smiled at her and looked friendly!

I'd also got close to my friend Katie, and we'd started hanging out at each other's houses. It was with this little friendship group that I'd hatched plans to go travelling after college and before we all settled down at uni.

We were making plans to visit America. It seemed that our spiritual home was California, especially as we were all fans of American TV, and so we were really excited about a cool trip over there. We hadn't got past the planning stage yet, but it was fun to chat about it, huddled together in the playground, giggling over the guys we might meet and how they'd love our English accents!

And I'd started my job in a local clothes store called Gossip in King's Lynn. It wasn't especially well paid, but it sold lots of well-known brands and it meant I was working in fashion. It was a start, and I loved the feeling of independence it gave me, earning a bit of my own money to spend on beauty and hair products and stylish clothes. I felt like I was heading somewhere, starting to live my own life after a couple of difficult years in the shadow of my school life.

I was on the brink of adulthood. That's when the accident happened, on a normal Saturday when thousands of teenagers across the country would be hanging out with their mates, going for drives or slouching around the shops in whichever town centres they hung out in. But for me, it had all changed. Forget the girl with Busted posters in her room, rows of heeled shoes and trendy jeans and invites to parties.

That was all gone – for now, at least. And in its place was that disgusting wheelchair.

Please don't think me ungrateful. I know I sound like a bit of a brat, hating the chair when everyone was being so kind, helping me to get in it and start moving my recovery forward. I was so grateful to them all. It was just that, I guess, I was moving from shock into a place of anger. I couldn't escape the effect of my injuries even for a moment, and now this wheelchair threatened to make a mockery of my debility – or that was how I saw it.

Before the crash I could've achieved anything, yet now all I would be was a freak. That's how it seemed to me at the time. I wish I'd known then how wrong I was. I wish I'd known that everything I wanted to achieve was possible, due to my absolute refusal to give up the girl I once was and the dreams I once had just because I was quadriplegic.

I had been in a state of trauma since the accident, but that state of mind was turning to outrage, and the wheelchair became my focus for it. I suddenly felt consumed by rage – a storm of pure, unadulterated, visceral fury.

Luckily for me, I was with Mum, who, by the harassed look on her face, could see I was about to explode.

'Jordan, sugar, you know that this is only the first step, right? This is your ticket to independence, and I can see it is really painful for you right now, but things will get better once you learn to get in a chair and move yourself about.

'This isn't how it'll be forever. Come on, darling, I know my positive, happy daughter is still in there. You have every right to be angry with the cards life has dealt you, but you can't change any of it right now.

'This chair, as horrible and as vile as it is, is the key to your future, and yes, it's hideous, it's monstrous, but you have to do this . . . You've worked so hard the last weeks to get ready for today. Don't give up now, just when things are starting to change.'

Mum smiled over at me. She always knew what to say to me; she still does.

'Aargh, sorry, Mum, I know you're right – you always are!' I managed a laugh. 'Go on then, let's get me in there. At least when I'm in it I won't be able to see it!'

'That's the spirit,' Mum grinned, and she nodded to the nurse and another male nurse who had joined us. Together, the nurses hoisted me into the chair and my body crumpled into it, drooping like a little rag doll.

It was so weird. I couldn't hold my body up at all. Everything about me was so weak. Even though there was the wide back of the chair to support my head, I leant against Mum and she held me in place while the room spun.

'Oh, I feel so dizzy, don't move yet,' I groaned.

'Don't worry, we're not going anywhere until you're ready. This is a big day; it's huge, Jordan. You're mobilising at last.'

Mum's voice was steady. It calmed me.

'Well, I will once the room has stopped spinning! Gah, I feel awful,' I moaned, yet despite feeling sick as a dog and as weak as a kitten, I can't deny I felt a small thrill finally to be upright. I knew Mum was right. This was the start of the next part of my journey, and I knew deep down I was eager to embrace it.

'Oh, lovely, we'll wait here,' said Mum, and we did, for another ten minutes until I felt ready to be moved. Mum pushed off gently, gliding me out of my room and into the wider ward. As we passed a mirror in the ward, I made the mistake of glancing at it, and was struck by the sight of a pale, sickly-looking girl in a huge black wheelchair. I can't deny it – I burst into tears.

It was a shock, seeing myself. I looked tiny. I'd lost so much weight. I felt constantly queasy so had to carry a sick bowl on my lap. My roots were brown, my highlights were growing out and I was wearing no make-up and just some comfortable, casual clothes: a grey T-shirt and jogging bottoms, despite the heat. In other words, I didn't look like Jordan at all!

I guess at that moment I could've plunged into some kind of depression, or been so bitter I turned within myself to a place I may not have found it easy to get back from. But once my tears had dried, I turned my face cautiously to the sun. I concentrated on the strange new feeling of movement, the slight breeze against my face, the new sights and sounds on the ward. Before I knew it I was humming a Busted song I liked, the sun was streaming into the bright ward, and I realised my first trip in my own chair may not have been a resounding success, but it was definitely a new beginning.

'Barbie Katie, you came!'

'Course I did, lovely! Couldn't wait to see you. How's things? How's your chair?' Katie screamed as she entered my room, throwing her bag on the floor and sitting cross-legged on the chair next to me.

'It looks like . . . like something Frankenstein might sit in!' I replied.

Katie had gorgeous long blonde hair and a wicked smile. She was always so upbeat, like me, and we could never work out why most people seem to spend so much time moaning about their lives!

She had visited several times, and we'd grown even closer as a result. Katie was really my best friend by now, certainly the one who came to see me most often. The first time she saw me was only days after the accident, when the metal halo contraption had been fitted to my head and my body had swelled up due to the trauma of the crash.

I'll never forget the first time she walked onto the ward. She took one look at me and collapsed. Fell down right there on the floor. We all gasped, wondering what the hell had happened.

From the floor she shouted up: 'It's OK, I'm OK. I'm here, Jordan, I'm here!'

With that, Mum and I burst out laughing. It was the one and only time I really belly-laughed in those first days. Trust Katie to do something hilarious!

Even now it makes me cackle to think of that moment, and how, even in the pit of despair when everything seemed to be lost, there was a brilliant friend making me laugh.

Katie arriving all the way from King's Lynn was a treat. I'd been so excited that she was coming to see me for a couple of days. I couldn't wait to show her my nifty moves in my monster chair. I'd even managed to push myself a little, though I didn't get far as my arms were way too feeble yet, but I was proud of even that small triumph.

'Frankenstein chair, yes, I know! That's exactly what I said the first time I saw it! Sooo great to see you.' I giggled.

'So, how's it going? Any fit doctors?' She chuckled.

'Well, now you mention it, the new consultant is quite good-looking. Married, though, so off limits . . . ha, ha, ha.' For those next days I knew I'd feel like a 'normal' teen again.

Over those two days we chatted about all the usual things teenage girls talk about: who had got with whom, who was cheating on whom. The usual kind of stuff. It was like old times. Katie perched on my bed and we watched *Mean Girls* on the television, discussing Lindsay Lohan's hair and make-up.

It was Katie who first noticed that my hair hadn't been highlighted, despite my mum's insistence that she could get a hairdresser to come in. I had said I wanted it done as a reward for getting into the wheelchair, but at the time I'd felt too dizzy. I hadn't mentioned it again; I don't know why, as I had always been very sensitive to my hair looking OK, and even though I didn't know Katie *that* well, she already knew that about me.

'I love Mum to bits, but she's rubbish at doing my hair,' I laughed. 'She always puts it in plaits, so I haven't bothered having it styled. What's the point, anyway, as I'm stuck in here . . .' My voice trailed off.

I suddenly felt quite vulnerable and wasn't sure why, though I knew I carried a sense of being 'different' since the accident. I hadn't wanted even to think about trying to make myself pretty again, even though I'd been upset when I caught sight of myself. I'd shut that part of my identity off, perhaps thinking I'd never look 'pretty' again as I'd always be in a wheelchair.

I didn't know it, but I was hiding my feelings even from myself. I didn't know how I could look attractive again, how I could possibly make myself look better. What was the point making an effort, because I'd always, always be quadriplegic.

Katie looked at me for a second.

'Hmmm . . . are you sure that's the reason?' she said. We'd grown very close, very quickly, and already she knew when I wasn't being entirely truthful.

'OK, OK, I just don't feel like me any more, and I just don't know if I'll ever be able to straighten my own hair again, so why bother? It's less painful just to leave it in the past. I hate everyone having to do everything for me. I can't eat by myself. I can't drink by myself. I can't even wash myself. What's the point in getting someone else to do my hair, knowing they'll always do it wrong?'

With that, I lapsed into silence. I'd been through enough. Perhaps I'd never be truly myself again.

'Rubbish!' said Katie stoutly. 'I have never met a more stubborn, determined person than you, Jordan. If you can't work out how to style your long hair, then you're right, no one can, but I'm going to try!'

With that, Katie called for one of the nurses, and she fished my straighteners out of the drawer next to my bed. Mum had brought them to the hospital in the hope I'd want my hair done at some point.

I felt a sudden lump in my throat.

When Katie had arrived, Mum had popped out to do some shopping and have a breather from being stuck inside the ward all day. When she returned, I greeted her by saying that I wanted to take her up on her offer of a hairdresser, and within a few days I had blonde streaks again highlighting my hair.

I'd concealed my deepest fears about my looks, about whether I'd ever properly reclaim my identity, from everyone, including myself.

When I use concealer now, I'm pretty liberal with the product. I like the feeling of covering up the bits of me that I want covered, being able to make a choice about what I show and what I hide.

I use a brush and paint a triangle under my eyes to hide my dark circles. Then I swap to a make-up sponge, slightly damp, to pat the concealer onto my skin. But that's where the work of hiding features stops. For me, concealer then becomes a way of highlighting, such as the downward-facing triangle of concealer on my forehead that I paint to enhance it, creating a lighter area, bringing it forward.

Then I paint concealer down the sides of my nose to define them – again it's a process of sculpting my features for best effect. Then I paint a blob of concealer on my cupid's bow above my lip to emphasise that small dip, and on my chin, highlighting, defining and shaping.

Using the concealer brush or beauty blender, I blend it all into my foundation base, taking care not to leave any lines or smudges.

To me, using concealer in make-up is always a positive process, a way of creating the look I want and literally drawing the eye to areas I like and making other areas recede a little. It is a way of being in control of my best features, and yes, it is like creating the confidence to look boldly back at a world that cannot stop staring. When I'm wearing it, I feel a stronger, more in-control person, ready to take on the world and live my part in it.

In life, concealing is a more elusive behaviour. Concealing can be a way of hiding our true selves from those around us, for fear we won't be loved or accepted for who we really are. Yet we can only ever be ourselves. In fact, that is our true mission in life, I believe: to become absolutely our best version of who we are.

Make-up gives me the best version of myself, but it isn't the answer to everything – nothing is that powerful!

Instead, it is part of our emotional toolbox. It is one of the things I can call on to boost my self-esteem and connect with who I am by looking (and therefore, feeling) the way I want to. It's so easy to fall into the trap of being who other people want us to be: friends, parents, partners, they all have expectations of us.

And that's OK; there's nothing wrong with compromise and working together, but it must never be at the expense of your true identity. I don't know what floats your boat – whether it's dance, music, art, sport or science that makes you feel great and makes you who you are. Your task, like mine, is to find the thing that makes you unique, your passion in life, because without it, who are you?

I know I concealed a lot from my mum and family during my time in hospital. I hid my darkest emotions, and fears, because it was a way of protecting them all. I'm glad I did it. They were going through enough without me adding to their burdens, and I know they hid their feelings from me as well. It must've been a huge wrench for Mum, leaving Eden with Darren all week and only seeing her at weekends. She must've been torn to pieces emotionally.

She has only ever conceded that recently, now that my life has become amazing. She never did then, and I totally respect her decision.

My confidence increased almost immediately on having my hair highlighted again. It was only a small glimmer of blonde, but it made me feel more *me*. When I saw my reflection the next time I was pushing myself around the ward, someone who wasn't a complete stranger looked back at me. I was in the process of finding myself again.

I was also making new friends.

The rigorous physio had strengthened my arms to the point where I could now pretty much push myself around the ward as often as I wanted, although I was incredibly slow as it took so much effort to do each push.

Another sign that my old self was returning was the fact that I struck up conversations with other patients, I'd go and chat to the old ladies and people would stop by my bed. I felt like a little chick hatching from a shell, pecking through the thin membrane, noticing the sharpness as I cracked through the final barrier to take lungfuls of air.

I'd hidden away in my side room (because I was fifteen I couldn't be on the adult ward), but my growing mobility meant I had to interact. It forced me outward.

I got chatting to a young woman in her late teens who could not get out of bed. Her name was Kim, and she was an Asian girl who'd contracted a virus during her pregnancy, though she eventually recovered enough to walk out of the hospital.

Kim seemed to know what she wanted. She had a feisty attitude to being in hospital. She definitely wasn't a victim of her condition, and was a bit of a character on the ward.

I was instantly drawn to her after I saw her joking with the nurses, one of them bending over with laughter.

'What's the joke?' I smiled, wheeling myself up to her bedside.

'Oh, nothing, don't mind me,' she said, flat on her back, 'I can't even see you properly but my name's Kim. What's yours?'

'Hey, I'm Jordan,' I replied.

'Well, don't worry, I'm not going to ask you how you got into that godawful chair. Tell me, which of the doctors do you think is the best-looking?

'Oh, I've already had this conversation with my friend Katie; we've got them all sussed out. Now which ones do you want, the single or the married?' I snorted, before screwing up my eyes in pretend concentration.

'Well, it has to be . . .' and I named one of the younger junior doctors.

'Ha, he was my choice too. Fight you for him! Well, I would if I could get out of bed!' she tossed back at me. I liked her instantly.

We got on so well that one evening we asked the nurses to push my bed over to hers so we could have a 'sleepover'. Yay, I was being a 'normal' teenager again!

We giggled and chatted about our lives, creating the immediate intimacy that so often comes with people who know what it is to have been through something life-changing.

I also made friends with an eighteen-year-old guy, Matt, who had lost the use of his legs in a car accident. He later became a champion sport shooter and won gold at the 2008 Paralympics in Beijing and bronze in the London Paralympics in 2012. He was also picked for the GB1 squad for the 2016 Rio Paralympics! It just shows what people can do if they push through the tough times.

It was great to speak to patients rather than the constant stream of different nurses and doctors. Together, we felt like a gang, hanging out as if we were choosing to be together. We didn't talk about our accidents. We chatted, laughed, told jokes and wound each other up, just like real life. We didn't waste time talking about our injuries; it was too much of a mood-breaker. We just had a laugh together.

In some ways, the hospital was like a protective bubble, though I wouldn't find this out till later. Inside the ward we weren't stared at; we were the 'normal' ones.

For the first time, hospital felt like home, like a kind of sanctuary. I started carrying my make-up bag with me on my lap when I went round the ward, stopping at the nurses' station for a chat, just sitting there holding the thing like a talisman. Having my hair done had made me dream that one day I might even put my own make-up on again, however crazy that seemed.

I kept that vision quiet. I wasn't ready to share it, but the thought seeded somewhere in my brain, pointing the way to my happiness, though I didn't yet know it.

7

Definition

Creating My Own Life

'Always be bold enough to define your own life. Don't let others,
or your problems or situation, define it for you.'

'I want to spend my birthday at home.'

The day I said that to my consultant felt huge, really
momentous. I was starting to define my wishes, to make my
own decisions about my recovery after months of being a
passive patient, and it felt good to know my own mind.

'Look, it's still summertime; that means I've got until
October to become strong enough to be discharged. That
gives me two whole months.'

I looked at Mum's face as I spoke. I could see her love for
me in her eyes, but also some anxiety.

Leaving hospital would be a big step, the biggest so far.
Would I be ready? I had no idea, but I knew I was going to

try. After all, I'd seen my class from school a couple of weeks earlier, when they came to see me. I'd managed fine with that. In fact, I'd really enjoyed seeing them, chatting about our area and about school. Surely things weren't going to be *that* different on my return. I might need a bit of help, but Mum could do that, couldn't she?

The consultant looked over at Mum. She sat in her chair next to me, fiddling with a ring. For a moment she wouldn't meet my eye.

'Jordan, hon, it's a big decision, and I'm glad you want to come home, and yes, of course we've all missed you, but make sure you're not pushing yourself too hard.'

'You're probably worried about me because I freaked out a bit at seeing my chair. I'd set my heart on mobilising, and when it didn't go to plan I got upset. I understand why that could make you fret about me, but, honestly, I'm sick of being in hospital now – no offence, doctor – and I miss everyone at home so much. I need to know I can go home, and I want to be there with my family on my birthday. Please just say yes – it'll mean the world to me.'

Mum's eyes filled with tears. She didn't have to say anything. The consultant nodded over at me, and I beamed. I was going home for my sixteenth, and I could finally get on with living my life – or so I thought.

The people that surround you are often important to how you perceive yourself. When my class came to see me earlier in the summer, it was the first time the majority of them would see me in a wheelchair. I was nervous about the visit, and didn't sleep well (do I ever?) the night before.

That changed when I saw them. It was a balmy summer day, and so we all decided to have a picnic.

Suddenly I was a regular teenager again.

'Hey, guys, I can't believe you're here!' I could move my right arm enough to give a small version of a wave.

'Hey, Jordan! How's it going?'

'Hey, Jordan, God, how are you? Are you OK now? When are you coming home?'

'Will you be able to come back to school?'

I was bombarded with questions from curious class-mates. No one seemed at all phased by my ugly chair, and I soon settled into chatting and laughing as everyone pulled out sandwiches and lemonade.

Katie had already been visiting me when they arrived, and I could feel her solid presence next to me throughout the afternoon. She is always pretty protective of me. One of the guys from my year handed me a box to open, and without a second thought Katie lunged over and unwrapped it, to save me any awkwardness over my inability to do it myself.

The class had bought me a pair of pink Converse train-ers, knowing how fond I was of that colour.

I was very touched, and spent the rest of the day thanking people. Later I sat in bed, when everyone had left, with the

Converse. I felt happy that I'd seen everyone, and that they'd treated me like they used to, but I also felt sad that the shoes would never get worn down. I would never have to throw them out because I'd walked or run them into the ground. They'd stay as pristine as they were on that day, because I couldn't ever walk in them. Even now, years on, I still have that pair of shoes and they look immaculate.

Seeing them all leave had also been hard. I couldn't imagine that kind of freedom now. They all climbed back into the bus, waving and hollering, and then off they went, back to their lives, their fun and their futures. I knew it would do me no good to dwell on those thoughts.

I did have an insight, though, that made me feel a little sad. I realised I knew no one who had had the same injury; no one who could guide me in how I was supposed to feel going through all this; no one to reassure me that things would get better, and no one to share the shitty times when my sense of all the things I'd lost by being involved in that car crash threatened to overwhelm me.

That's when I decided I had to be my own inspiration in order to move on with my life. I had no one to look up to or to mentor me. I had a moment of clarity, a defining thought that told me *I* would have to be that inspiration, and that I had to start right now.

Despite my feelings, the day had been a success, and I felt reassured that everything to do with school, friends and my social life would stay the same when I returned. Those things were really important to me. My social life was a big part of who I was as well.

To help me catch up with the school I had missed last term, the hospital had organised a teacher to come in every day to teach me maths, science and English lessons.

Honestly, as if life wasn't bad enough!

Imagine having a profound and devastating injury, and then having to memorise equations! Surely the one 'perk' of being this ill would be not to have to sit through the kind of lessons I hated at school anyway. I was never good at maths, and watching the poor man, who must have been quite elderly, scrawl on the whiteboard provided for him almost drove me to distraction. Several times I actually hid from him by making my way to another part of the hospital. I suppose at least I was able now to prove I was getting stronger by my ability to bunk off lessons!

Then inspiration struck.

It came in the form of a new student nurse who had started on our ward.

'Hi, Jordan, I'm here to tell you about the next occupational therapy session. Can I join you?'

I looked up and saw a glamorous young woman, with mascara so thick it looked like false eyelashes and hair swept up in a stylish chignon. She looked amazing.

For a moment I didn't speak, and then the words gushed out of me: 'Wow, you look fab! I love your mascara – I used to wear mine really heavily like that. I love that look.'

'What do you mean, used to? Why aren't you wearing it now? If you want, we can talk about OT later and I'll put some on you. You've got a gorgeous face, and lovely thick lashes. Where's your make-up bag? Let's do it!' the nurse chuckled, and put down her clipboard.

'It's in there. Don't look at all the crap I've got in that cupboard. Yes, that's it, in there, fish it out. The mascara might be a bit clumpy; I haven't worn it for weeks now.'

Excitement rose up inside me. The nurse pulled out the wand, but before she did, she held my small beauty mirror up to my face. I don't know why she did that; perhaps to show me a 'before' and 'after' view. I saw my own colourless reflection staring back at me, noticing how I seemed to recede into the background.

Make-up has always meant much, much more than mere vanity to me. It was a way of expressing my creativity and lust for life, for gaining the self-confidence I lacked as a child and young girl. It defined who I was, and without it I suddenly felt lost.

The nurse must have noticed my reaction.

'Come on, let's get working. You're going to look gorgeous when I've finished with you,' she said kindly.

She started stroking the creamy liquid onto my lashes. When she'd finished, she held up my small beauty mirror for me to admire my reflection.

'I look like "me" again!' I squealed with happiness.

'You're a beautiful girl, Jordan, you need to remember

that. You can be quadriplegic and glamorous. There's no note that says otherwise!' With that, she sashayed off, exaggerating her movements and making me laugh. My spirits were high for the whole of that day.

Later the physio and occupational therapy session took place in the OT kitchen, where we were all relearning our cooking skills. Usually the sight of a roomful of disabled people like myself struggling to use the knives or forks on our hand straps to chop vegetables or eat the dinner we managed to cook, made me despondent. I often tried to bunk off those lessons as well. I hated seeing my own feeble, pointless efforts mirrored by the others. But that day was different.

A few of the others, including Kim, noticed my make-up and commented, saying I was looking good. I stayed with the class this time, chopping mushrooms for a veggie lasagne we were making together, not minding as the guy next to me dropped the carrot he'd been hacking at, needing an OT therapist to reach down and pick it up for him.

That day I chatted with everyone, enjoying their company, because somewhere inside me a flame had been relit, a passion reignited. It was a tiny seed of hope, like a small candle flame bobbing in the darkness.

Then the next day, the pivotal moment happened. It isn't an exaggeration to say that this was the point where everything came together for me. More important, perhaps, than the crash and its effects.

One of the guys on the ward lost his food strap. That was the band that fitted around your hand to hold a knife or a fork. So, without thinking, I gave him mine. That day I started holding a fork, getting the nurse to put it between my thumb and forefinger, and in so doing, I discovered a way to actually feed myself, using my own normal fork and not that awful strap.

That was the light bulb moment for me.

When I realised I could hold a fork, I thought, why not my mascara wand? Why not a foundation brush or a lipstick?

Suddenly my future seemed a million times brighter. Up to that point my days were defined by ward rounds, wash times and mealtimes. Now I saw that I could use my time to practise.

I sat at the nurses' station all day, every day, asking them to open my make-up bag and take out the mascara, unscrewing the wand for me and handing me the black-tipped applicator. For the first hundred times I instantly dropped it, swearing as the wand bounced down over my grey T-shirt and joggers, leaving a trail of black smears. Each time I had to wait till a nurse was free so I could ask him or her to pick it up again and put it back in my scrunched-up fingers. I kept going. I swore a lot in those days!

My hands were both permanently pulled into tightly balled fists by my spinal cord injury. I had to work out a way to hold the applicator between the gaps in my fingers, the parts that were almost fused together but not quite.

On and on I went, trying countless times until I managed to hold it almost steady. I let out a whoop of joy, and with a shaking arm, I tried to utilise the small amount of movement I had in my arm to bring my hand nearer to my face. By now I could move my neck forward a little, and so I bent towards it, willing the mascara brush to touch my eyelashes. It took several more goes before they made contact, days of painstaking repetition, with only my will driving me on.

Once they made contact, I didn't know what to do. I couldn't move my arm from right to left to apply the mascara, so instead I moved my face, hoping to press the black paint onto my lashes. Needless to say, I ended up looking like I had black eyes, but it started to work, and the more times I persevered, the less messy and more 'normal' it looked.

This small victory gave me more than hope; it gave me definition. In make-up terms, definition is part of sculpting the face, redesigning the natural look to create a more polished appearance. We define our lips with lip pencil and our brows with pomade or brow pencil. Products are used to emphasise each feature, carving out its place in the look as a whole.

My life had been formed into a new shape and texture by my injury, yet I didn't let this define me entirely.

By reclaiming my ability to apply make-up, I wasn't just making myself look nicer, it was way more profound than that. It was a way of redefining my expectations about myself, and perhaps how I use make-up to redefine other people's perceptions of disability and serious injury such as mine, though that was yet to come. I loved make-up before the crash, but at this point it became symbolic of a need to control something in my life. I couldn't control much else!

Suddenly I was back in charge of something. I knew that if I found a way to make my body work enough to put on my products, then I was forging my identity again; I wasn't defeated by the crash and everything that followed.

I progressed to asking the nurses just to open my make-up bag, so that I could attempt to scoop out the mascara brush from it, using my closed-up hands.

It was incredibly frustrating, at times making me weep with tiredness, at other times making me connect back to that deep rage at being in the position I was in through no fault of my own. The most important thing about it all was that no matter how I felt, I carried on. I knew deep down that this was the key to my future.

Choosing your own path can be tough. We all have times when we face obstacles and challenges. We can either overcome them, work round them or give up. Only you can know which option to take, but the rewards of not giving up, when it is something important to you, are priceless.

I was fighting for my sense of self, though I didn't know it. With each and every dropped applicator grew a fiercer and fiercer conviction that I had to keep going. I tapped into something inside me, and you can too. You can define your own life by deciding what makes you happy and going for it. You are the only one who can push yourself to achieve the things you want to in life, and you *can* do it. Next time you hesitate or question yourself, think of me, alone at that nurses' station, grappling with an unthinkable task – a paralysed girl trying to put on her own make-up.

However much it scared me to fail, I knew I had to try, and keep trying. It seemed like a natural progression for me. Suddenly I had something concrete to aim for, that was entirely of my own devising.

Looking back, I don't know how I had the courage, but I refused to give way completely to this condition. I refused to let the anger, the frustration, get the better of me. I knew the only way forward was with a positive, can-do attitude, with force of will and with the scrapings of self-belief that were left after everything that happened. It was time to start fighting for the life I wanted.

Learning to apply make-up after my accident was one of the most pivotal things I've ever done. Before the accident, I *loved* make-up. It was a way for me to express myself, to show the world who I wanted to be.

After the accident, due to the paralysis in my hands and the lack of strength and mobility in my arms, I was unable to apply it. I willed my arms to have the strength to move up to my face to apply mascara.

The perseverance it took to reclaim this activity, that had

seemed so simple before, proved to me that my disability didn't have to define my future. I was able to teach myself how to hold make-up tools in a way that works for me. I've mastered it to the point where I've since refused to wear a hand splint, which acts to stretch my hands out, because I need them to stay scrunched up so that I can 'grip'.

Make-up products define my features, making them bolder or brighter. That's how I saw this part of my recovery. I was redefining myself, making myself bolder and brighter, and by relearning to apply my beauty products, I was colouring in my life again.

8

Blush

Turning Things Around

'Always turn a negative into a positive.'

'Hey, guys, it's so great you're here! I can't wait to get going!' I greeted my family, mum Jane, sister Eden, Mum's partner Darren, Auntie Jackie, her partner Uncle Fred and cousin Pru as they arrived on the ward. Today was a big milestone: my first trip out into the 'real' world, beyond the confines of the hospital.

'Hello, sugar, the taxi's waiting and we're all hungry!' laughed Mum as she swooped down to kiss me, her eldest daughter, gently on my forehead.

'And you've got your make-up on! Go, girl!' said Auntie Jackie.

I was thrilled they had noticed. I didn't have much make-up on. I still wasn't proficient enough at handling things to really go for it, but I'd managed mascara that wasn't too 'panda eyes', and a bit of blush because I'd found I could grip the thicker blusher brush quite well.

'You look beautiful, lovely, almost back to your old self,' said Fred kindly. I knew I looked ill, despite the fact that I'd been able to sit in the sun on my balcony.

That had become a daily pleasure – just sitting and closing my eyes, listening to the hum of the air extractors and feeling as close to serene as I had since the accident.

Now that I had a goal for my discharge date, I seemed able to relax more.

'Well, let's go then, I'm famished. The food in here is rotten!' Everyone laughed at that.

Mum took hold of the wheelchair grips and steered me out of my room and down through the ward, Eden skipping along in front wearing a gorgeous new pink dress mum had bought specially for my big 'going out' day. I gave a few waves as we passed patients and the nurses on their rounds.

Out in the sunlight, I blinked. Even though I had done a little sunbathing, I was still unprepared for the sensation of being outside again. At first I felt panicky as we moved further away from the hospital grounds, towards the waiting taxi that would take us to TGI Fridays near the Meadowhall Shopping Centre.

'Aargh, my chair feels all wobbly, like I might topple over! It's weird!' I was laughing as I said it, but I felt anxious. The pavement leading to the taxi was uneven and my chair seemed to lurch rather than roll towards the vehicle. I hadn't given the taxi ride much thought, but as we approached, I suddenly felt even more nervous. This would be my first car ride. Why hadn't I realised this was actually a big deal?

The cab was a wheel-on one and so I sat inside, in my chair, in the back, which felt weird. I felt my breath come in shorter, sharper gasps and I realised I might be having a panic attack.

'It's OK, Jordan, we won't be in here long. We knew this might be tricky, but we're all here for you. If it's too much we don't have to go; we can go to the hospital canteen and eat there. It's up to you. Whatever is best for you.'

Mum leant over and touched my cheek, stroking it gently. Her lovely face was filled with concern and I couldn't bear giving her more to worry about.

'I'm fine. I need to do this. Come on, let's just go,' I said as firmly as I could manage.

'That's my brave girl,' answered Mum, settling back into her seat and strapping herself in. Even the clunk of the seat belt made me wince.

As the car built up speed, I stared straight ahead. I didn't pray – at least I don't think that's what I was doing – but in my mind I repeated over and over *keep us safe, keep us safe* until we pulled up outside the restaurant.

I was wheeled out onto the pavement. As Mum pushed me inside, the lyrics *I could run but the feeling is there / No place anywhere can hide me* popped into my head, looping round and round like an incantation.

Today it had renewed significance: 'no place anywhere can hide me' summed up how it was to be a wheelchair user as diners looked up from their food to watch me as we made our way to our table. I guess they felt pity or concern, or even just plain curiosity at the sight of me huddled in my Frankenstein chair. I felt the stares as much as I saw them. I could not hide my disability. It was there on public display, and this was my first experience of it.

Then we realised that my chair wouldn't fit under the restaurant table, so I had to sit slightly away from everyone, a move that I struggled not to feel isolated with.

The menu had one vegetarian choice, a vegetable fajita, so I had to order that, while everyone around me tucked into burgers and fries. My contentment at being with everyone was turning to a feeling of exclusion, though nobody was to blame – it was just how it was.

My shock and anger following the crash were morphing into a rejection of its effects, a rejection of my limitations. That had worked in a good way with my fight to apply my make-up. I rejected the fact that my hands didn't work, my arms were weak and I couldn't move my body, and I used what mobility I did have to forge my own way of holding brushes, using my teeth to navigate and position them in my useless hands.

But that day, I announced at the table that I wanted to

go shopping in the mall. Looking back, I was nowhere near ready to enter the fray, so this decision was clearly a repudiation of my new disabled status.

Mum and Jackie glanced at each other. I knew by that look that they thought I wasn't ready, and it only made me want to go more.

Mum turned to me and said, 'Are you sure you want to? It's crowded out there, and you look pale. I'm worried this is all too much for you.'

Mum was right in that I'd started to look unwell. My neck was hurting me, and in response my body was coated in a cold sweat that rendered me clammy and uncomfortable.

I didn't know it at the time as it hadn't been diagnosed, but I was also suffering from a condition called autonomic dysreflexia (AD), a potentially life-threatening condition of acute hypertension suffered by people with spinal cord injury.

Symptoms include the severe sweating I was experiencing, high blood pressure, headaches, anxiety and flushed skin. If left untreated, or not recognised, as mine wasn't for several months following the accident, it can cause seizures, kidney failure, cerebral haemorrhage and even death. It is serious, but we had no idea I was afflicted by it. I assumed it was a symptom of my injury and there was nothing I could do about it.

By the end of the meal I felt shattered, but wouldn't give up on my quest. Mum wheeled me through the shopping centre. Everywhere there was activity and noise: people chatting, walking, sauntering, arguing, shouting even. Loud music pumped from some of the shops, while a group of teenagers jostled and joked with each other.

The shops seemed too bright, their lights streaming out, hurting my eyes. A mother with two small children passed by, one of the kids screaming, the other wailing, and I wanted to clutch my ears. It was too much; a sensory overload. It seemed loud and overwhelming with the number of people.

Despite that, I was still determined to go inside the shops. I used to love going shopping with my friends, spending our Saturday-job money on new clothes or shoes, especially if we had a party or sleepover to go to. But this was so different. In reality, I was intensely vulnerable, a severely disabled young woman who was living out the most sensitive time in her teenage years, when having a sense of identity and her self-image were crucial. Yet I didn't want to acknowledge it, or accept it, that day.

As Mum wheeled me into one of the brightly lit clothes shops, I was starting to feel very unwell and shaky. By now you probably know that I have a stubborn streak! It is what has got me so far today, but that day it drove me way beyond my limits. I felt defiant, having been the object of the stares in the restaurant, and so I vowed to carry on doing the things I used to love in spite of how ill and helpless I felt.

Two teenage boys whooped next to me. The house music in the shop we'd turned into was booming in my ears. I became acutely conscious of my unfashionable clothing, the sweat staining my T-shirt, my huge black chair that wouldn't fit down the clothes aisles.

I gazed with blank eyes at the rows and rows of tops and dresses, trying to make sense of them, feeling more alienated by the second. *I'll never be able to wear jeans again. I won't ever wear heels or a pretty dress*, was all I could think.

'Let's go, Mum,' I muttered, and we turned to leave the store.

As Mum wheeled me out of the shop I caught a glance of my reflection in the shop doors. I saw a frail, sickly, ill girl in a huge, monstrous wheelchair. I looked a shadow of my former self; a trace as thin as smoke. What was I thinking, being here, trying to be normal? I wasn't ready to re-enter the world I'd lost, and in that moment I knew it.

The realisation hit me forcefully.

'Take me home, please,' I said. It was the last thing I said until I was back in my hospital bed. I was fifteen years old, the age at which I was most sensitive about my appearance. I was already insecure after the bullying I'd experienced at school. This felt like the final injury, the worst of all. I saw myself as I really was, and all illusions of that girl who loved shopping and beauty fell from me in that moment of recognition. I would never be the same again. I would always be trapped inside my own damaged body. I was broken beyond repair, and I was deeply ashamed of myself. How would I ever become whole again?

I've called this chapter 'Blush' because it reminded me of that shame, that feeling of blushing about myself. How awful is that? I was ashamed to be me at that point. I really had no idea that I would ever live and enjoy life again. Everything felt crap. Everything.

In that moment, I hated myself. I hated how I looked, how broken my body was, how *incapable* I was. Yet I survived, and actually I've learnt how to thrive by turning things around, making positives out of negatives and holding onto my dreams for myself relentlessly.

I know now that it's completely natural to feel that shame about yourself, especially about the broken bits of yourself, and yet those parts can be the most fragile and beautiful. Today I've learnt to cherish the damaged parts of me, body and soul, and to stop trying to fix them. This leaves me free to live my life in the best way I can.

What are you ashamed of? And can you forgive yourself for that shame?

It was a difficult day, a dark time. I could feel myself retreating into myself when I'd done so much to come forward. But it was a temporary blip, an essential 'regrouping', if you like, that eventually resulted in my complete acceptance of myself as I am, my damage and frailty included.

Now the only blushing I do is when I apply one of my gorgeous blush shades, from the hundreds of palettes I get sent by brands wanting me to endorse their products. (By the

way, I only ever promote brands I truly love – it's so important to keep my integrity.)

The shades I have range from delicate pinks to 'nude'
versions, to warmer, more orange tones, and I choose one
depending on my overall look: a brighter pink for a summer
look; a warm, orangey tone for an autumnal look. I love
applying blush in a great sweep, using it as a way of giving a
healthy, natural-looking glow to my cheeks.

I brush it back into my hairline over the foundation. The
warmth it leaves helps my complexion by adding colour, but
it also builds on the contouring, using optical illusion to
reshape that area of my face. Each time I apply it I think
of that pale girl in the reflection. I can barely recognise her
now, and each sweep of colour on my skin takes me further
away from her, though she is still always there inside me.

Today I honour her by acknowledging how fragmented
she felt, how lost, yet how she has overcome so much she
would never have thought possible.

It isn't the easiest task to reach up into where my skin
meets my hairline, though the strength in my arms has
increased with practice and time. I have had to learn tricks
to help me hold the brushes. I switch the angle of the brush
or the way I am holding it by using my teeth to reposition
the implement in my gnarled hands, as I mentioned earlier.

I guess if I'd have known then what I do now, that perseverance and determination bring success in even the hardest
tasks, I may not have felt so hopeless and defeated. But I

didn't know that one day I'd be shooting vlogs for YouTube, or giving make-up tutorials and talks at major London retail stores and beauty conferences.

It hadn't actually been the sight of me that made me want to leave the mall. It hadn't been the lights, noises or crowds that sent me back to my hospital bed, even though they felt overwhelming. It hadn't even been the overpowering scent of perfume from the shops or the beat of the music banging in my ears that had driven me out. It was the stares.

From the moment I left the hospital, wheeled into and out of the restaurant and through the mall, I was stared at by passers-by. I felt horribly exposed. And it was the pitying glances that stung the most. That's why I begged to go home even before I'd bought anything new.

That's why I wanted the safety of my bed, knowing that at least there I was surrounded by other patients and victims of accidents as bad, or even worse, than mine. I fitted in, and I didn't 'out there'.

I knew I'd been lucky to survive my injury. My life was saved by the skill of paramedics and surgeons, but I would have to get used to this new sensation, this new visibility, and fast. I wasn't ungrateful. I didn't wish myself dead. It was simply that I didn't know how to come to terms with my conspicuousness. Would people ever stop staring? And would I ever stop caring?

The next challenge was my first trip home to King's Lynn.

I was going for an entire weekend as a precursor to coming home for good in six weeks' time.

Two members of the occupational therapy team took me back home in a taxi. Again, it felt very strange to be inside a car, and quite scary.

The journey was uneventful except for feeling very long. I was desperate to get home, of course, but the added pressure came from the fact that I had to sit in the back seat. Again, I refused to sit behind the passenger seat, preferring the right side, behind the driver. As we ate up the miles, I hummed to myself until the guy driving turned to me and asked if I wanted the radio on.

'Radio One, please, that'd be great, thanks.' And so we listened as the car moved steadily closer to home. I literally couldn't wait to get there. It was the end of August 2005, and I'd been away for three months. It felt like forever.

After what seemed like an eternity, we reached the familiar streets of King's Lynn. Staring out of the window, everything looked the same, yet I was completely different. Looking out, seeing the same houses, roads and trees that I'd grown up around, I could hardly believe I was the same person returning. Yet as soon as we drew up outside our house, an old Victorian terrace in Gaywood Road, the front door was flung open and Eden dashed out, waving and shouting, 'Jordan!'

'Eden, hey, li'l sis, how are you, gorgeous girl?' I replied in a happy, sing-song voice. I was home at last. Everything felt better. I was taken out of the car on a slide board and, instead of going up the stairs, I was brought into our lounge instead.

Except it wasn't a lounge any more. The room had been split in two by a decorated screen, creating my 'bedroom'. A kind family friend had wallpapered the screen with a funky design, and had put a mirror on it with light bulbs round the edge for me to see myself clearly as I made myself up. Dominating my space was a hospital bed, which I was surprised to see.

I don't know what I was thinking, but I'd assumed I'd have my old room and bed back, but, of course, Mum couldn't keep carrying me up and down the stairs to get me up or put me to bed.

'Oh,' was all I said, feeling slightly dispirited to see that echo of hospital life.

'Sorry, sugar. We had to put you a bed and your things in here. Look, all your cushions and beauty things are down here. It won't be too bad, eh?'

Mum patted the bed. I was carefully placed in it, my neck supported to give me a rest. Lying back, I found it odd staring up at the front room ceiling, but I said nothing. I knew every nook and cranny in the house intimately, but not from this angle! Eden settled on the chair next to me with an array of Barbie dolls, some of which I recognised as my old ones.

'Look, Jordan, look at all my Barbies. This one is Holiday

Barbie, this one is . . .' Eden chatted happily next to me. It was lovely hearing her familiar voice, being back somewhere I knew so intimately.

'She's a beauty, I love her pretty dress. What about that one, what's she called?' I replied, knowing we would spend a happy evening together, running through everything I had missed while I'd been away.

From then on, friends arrived in a steady procession, some coming for a catch-up, others bringing pizza and staying all evening. I was exhausted. My neck was killing me, but I refused to go to sleep. I had waited for this moment and it had finally arrived, and I was determined to savour every last minute. Things actually felt 'normal' again, like things could carry on as they were before the accident, and all I'd need was a bit of extra help.

I felt positive. My spirits lifted, and I remember spending that weekend giggling as friends prattled on, messed about and generally showed me there was life after a wheelchair. Friendships have always been incredibly important to me. I'm naturally a really sociable person, and I love being surrounded by friends.

For that weekend, Mum was my carer, and it must've been hard for her as everything, including washing, dressing, eating, drinking and rolling me over at night, had to be done by her. But I could see she was thrilled for us all to be together again at home.

When the time came to get me in the car and drive me

back to Sheffield, I didn't feel upset. I was just really excited now to be coming home for my sixteenth birthday on 24 October.

Things felt good. I could now look forward to the next chapter of my life with renewed hope. Whatever faced me, I would get through it. I'd learnt so much about myself in hospital, my determination and my drive, and I knew I could find a way to be truly myself again, no matter the odds stacked against me.

The weather couldn't have been worse for the car journey back to Sheffield. This time Darren was driving, and Mum and me were in the car, with me sitting in the front. Torrential rain lashed against the windscreen for the whole three-hour drive. I was petrified. I think I sang all the way back to try and keep my thoughts occupied. I was frightened we'd have another crash, and nothing that Darren or Mum said could help. I think they were as worried as I was. I can't remember which songs I sang, but I know I didn't stop until we turned into the hospital car park.

Again, I felt ashamed of my fears. I felt like a child in that car, willing the journey to end and counting the minutes until we reached safety. Then it changed again. As the car stopped, and Darren turned to me and smiled, I felt a shot of pure gratitude. We'd survived. We were all safe and sound. My fears had been groundless, and I could breathe again.

Something about that journey stayed with me afterwards. Perhaps it was that feeling of thanks. The emotion started to spill over into other areas of my life, urging me forward and helping me to overcome the negative emotions such as embarrassment and fear.

I want to show you that it's possible to rise above that feeling of shame, even to celebrate the thing that makes you feel uncomfortable in your own skin. It isn't childish to feel scared or stupid, but it's what we do with those feelings that marks who we are and what we become. We can sink under them, or we can rise above them – it's our choice. My wheelchair and my disability are now my USPs, my Unique Selling Points, and I hope that inspires you to make positives out of your negatives, to turn things around in *your* life.

I welcome looks and stares today. I started my vlogs as a way of being completely open and transparent about my injuries, to demystify disability and to use it in a positive way, to share my battles with self-esteem and the ways I've overcome them in the hope that they inspire and motivate you guys to find your own true path through difficult feelings. I think that disability should be in the media more and I want to represent people who may feel that they are invisible because of their impairment. I want you to know that you can feel and look amazing too.

9

Highlight

Shining Bright

'Always highlight the positives in your life.'

The day came for me to leave hospital. It was 21 October 2005, three days before my sixteenth birthday.

I felt sad saying goodbye to my friends on the ward, and to the nurses I'd known for months. My funny mate Kim had left a couple of weeks earlier, so we'd already said our farewells and vowed to stay in touch. Kim was an incredible success story. She had recovered and had been able to stand before she left the ward, holding her toddler's hand, knowing she would walk freely by herself again. I don't know if that meant she was 'cured' of her illness, but it was strangely moving to see her standing independently, something most people are lucky enough to take for granted.

I hadn't been envious; I was just so happy for her, and I

was too excited about going home, properly. It felt like my life was restarting.

Mum gathered together all my cards and cuddly toys. They needed a huge bag just to fit them all in! It was that day I also learnt of some of the fundraising efforts that had been done for me in my community. Mum told me about some of the things people had done, and by the time she'd finished I was crying, I was so touched by everyone's efforts.

'Yes, so there was a blues night in a local pub to raise money for you, and I know that Springwood High had wristbands made by Jaz-D, the place you were going to do work experience at. They had your name on and your signature heart drawing. (I always used to sign my name replacing the 'o' with a heart; it was my thing, and I was so flattered they'd remembered that.)

'I think they were sold for a pound or two each to raise money for you. People have done so much, Jordan; they really love you.'

'And you too, Mum,' I replied, knowing that our community was rallying round in support of all of us as a family. I couldn't find the words then to thank people enough, and I still struggle today. It was an incredible feeling, going home, knowing that people were thinking of us still, after all the months I'd been in hospital.

My emotions were so mixed that day. By now my ward felt a bit like home, and I was really sad to leave, which is a bit contradictory because I'd been dying to leave!

At the same time, re-entering my world was scary, not least because Mum had had 'the chat' with me a couple of days earlier about the care I'd need at home. Even then I think I was deluded about my condition. I really believed that if I left hospital it would mean I was 'better', even though nothing had changed in terms of my mobility. I knew I'd be in a wheelchair for the rest of my life, barring some kind of medical miracle, but I thought I needed the care I did because I was in hospital, and that when I got home I'd be able to manage by myself. I didn't even realise my hands would always be paralysed.

Like I said – deluded!

I remember clearly the look on Mum's face as she sat next to me. I'd been writing a text, using the side of one of my thumbs to punch in the letters on my phone. I was getting pretty good at it, almost back to my pre-accident speed. She looked solemn, and instantly I asked what was wrong, thinking it must be something to do with Eden or one of my friends. Mum twirled a length of my long blonde hair as she spoke, a gesture that was at once comforting and intimate.

'Jordan, lovely, we need to have a chat about how it's going to be at home. The consultant came to see me, and he thinks you haven't quite grasped the extent of your injury in terms of its effects once you leave.'

'What do you mean? Won't you do it? We'll manage, won't we, Mum?' I answered, sipping my coffee through a straw, half an eye on the TV show on my monitor. 'I think I've got a pretty good idea, Mum. I'm paralysed for life; how much more do I need to know?' I said, not unhappily. I was just surprised that she needed to say it.

'I know that, Jordan, and you've been so brave. You're the most courageous person I know. I'm not saying that you don't understand, of course you do, but we need to talk about getting carers for you, and how many people we'll need on a daily basis. It's a lot to organise.'

'Carers?' I said, my face registering shock. I hadn't thought I'd need carers. 'But can't you do it, Mum, like you did when I came home for the weekend?'

Mum squeezed my right hand and kissed my forehead. It was a gesture of such love, such warmth, that I nearly burst into tears on the spot!

'I'll help you as much as I can, darling, but you are going to need round-the-clock care, and I can't give you that. I have Eden to look after as well, and I'm your mum, sweetie; I can't be your full-time carer as well, and I have to work.

'Sorry, but we need to work out what's best for you. You're coming home in a few days, and I want everything to be in place for you. I don't want you to come home and for us not to be prepared.'

I was silent for a moment as the news sank in. Carers? I knew what Mum was saying was true, but it was a shock, to say the least. When we leave hospital we're meant to be cured, aren't we? Well, perhaps not in my case, but somehow it hadn't occurred to me that all the things the nurses had to do to keep me clean, fed and generally looked after would now need to be done by someone else. Someone I didn't yet know. The thought of strangers moving me in the night and washing me every morning made me feel suddenly sick. I'd had enough of people pulling and prodding me. I yearned for privacy.

I put my phone down. 'So, what do we do?'

Mum sighed. 'We're going to need to find carers quickly, so I've made some enquiries and there is an agency locally we can use until we're able to hire people privately.

'The doctor says you'll need two people during the day to get you up and dressed, then one person overnight to turn you. Are you happy for me to organise that? If you're not happy with whoever it is that comes, we can look to changing them. This is just to get us through the first few weeks. So do I have your permission to call the agency?'

'OK, I understand. Yes, of course, Mum,' I replied, smiling into her eyes. I hated seeing her look so worried. 'It's fine, honestly. We just have to get on with it.' I made my smile as wide as possible, but I don't think I was very convincing because Mum patted my shoulder as she went off to make the call.

The prospect of people I didn't know touching me was pretty unpleasant. I'd got used to my nurses and the staff here. A couple of the nurses were a bit less sympathetic, but generally they were OK.

Before the operation I had been rolled to each side overnight to prevent bedsores. After the op, and once I was a little stronger, the night staff twisted my body, turning my hips to the side while keeping my top half stable, flat on my back, and relieving the pressure on my bottom. It was quite an art to do it properly and as unobtrusively as possible in the middle of the night. Would we find people I liked enough to be OK with this?

I spent the rest of the day in near silence, brooding over what Mum and the consultant had said. Surely it wouldn't be as bad as all that? Surely, in time, I'd regain a lot of my lost skills? I couldn't imagine a life where I couldn't grab myself a snack, or pop out to the shops.

As I said, the reality just wouldn't sink in, and so the next day I carried on as before, ignoring it, really, and concentrating on what meant the most to me, which was putting on my own make-up. Without the ability to do that, I really was lost.

Make-up has always meant more to me than just making myself pretty. It is an act of creation, almost like an artistic pursuit. I enjoyed painting and working on my features like an artist, creating subtle changes and enhancing the parts of me, like my eyes and cheekbones, that I like best.

The finished result is somehow never the point, though I like looking good – I'm the first to admit it! I enjoy the process, the application, choosing which 'look' I will go for each day, blending my moods with the products.

From the minute I wake up, I think, *which look to go for today?* How I feel is always the main driver for the make-up I apply, the look I create. If I feel confident I go for a bolder face, with smoky eyes and glamorous dark-stained lips.

If I feel quiet or just more peaceful, I go for a 'nude' look, with pared-down shades accenting my natural features and creating a look that could almost be taken for wearing no make-up at all.

Faces are generally the first things we look at. To me, they are the conduit of the soul, the mood of the person, their attitude to life, even. That's why doing my face has always been such a big deal. I have always wanted to present the image of my choice – one that is authentic to me – to highlight my confidence that day.

When I'm working through my beauty routine, highlight is one of the most important parts of the creation.

I use concealer to work in areas of light on top of my foundation, as I've said, but I also use a shimmery highlighter, which catches the light and makes a pretty glow on my skin. I mainly highlight my cheekbones to make them look more prominent. I love it. I use a smaller, more tapered brush than my foundation brush to swipe the powder, creating a thin veneer of shiny particles that finish off the effects of the more sculptural work I've already achieved with shadow and blush.

I also use brightening powder, which is quite similar,

but this acts on areas to stop them smudging and to keep make-up in place, to set the concealer. I use this under my eyes, bringing my brush as close to my face as I can and putting my head forward to 'embrace' the brush and its contents. I have this technique down to a fine art, as you've probably seen in my tutorials, and I can be incredibly accurate, placing the matte powder exactly where it needs to go, covering the dark circles under my eyes and helping my concealer to stay in place throughout the day.

It means the make-up under my eyes won't move, and I'll look like I've had eight straight hours of sleep! Luxury! I also use shimmery highlight on my cupid's bow to emphasise it, and on the bridge of my nose.

I had to be pushed all the way to the car, as I was still too weak to propel myself that far, especially on the carpeted areas of the hospital reception. The day was dull and rainy, yet I felt on cloud nine as Mum packed away my stuff in the boot (it's amazing how much you accumulate during a long hospital stay!). Our next-door neighbour was driving us all the way back home, illustrating yet again the kindness of the people we knew.

I thought I might shed a tear at leaving, but I felt impatient to go. I could almost taste my freedom. I just wanted to go home. I was desperate to get back to my family life, in my home, with my friends around me. However 'safe' the ward had been, I felt I was ready to leave now and start living again.

The drive felt shorter this time, but I still couldn't throw off my unease at being a passenger. This time I sat in the front and chatted as brightly as I could manage all the way back. These days I'm much more comfortable being in a car. I totally trust my fiancé Mike, and my mum, when it comes to driving me around, which really helps.

I was so focused on celebrating my birthday at home that nothing else really mattered, so I endured the journey, just so pleased to be going home, knowing I wouldn't have to be back there for a year for my first check-up.

Again my family greeted me with cuddles and kisses. Eden was beside herself with happiness to have me back with her, and I felt the same. I'd missed enough of her growing up; I was determined not to miss another day.

Mum settled me in my room that used to be the lounge. I was desperate to see my old bedroom upstairs, though, and so Darren carried me up. It was lovely seeing it again. All my things were there, as if I'd only walked out five minutes earlier, which felt strange. So much had happened since I was last in there on that fateful Saturday morning in May!

My big double bed was the same, with its lilac duvet cover and an array of mismatched cushions, which I loved. The walls were pink, and behind my bed, covered with posters of Busted. My books were all there, alongside my Winnie-the-Pooh phone, my make-up case filled with eyeshadow shades, bottles of perfume and different brands of foundation and blusher, with a mirror inside. I loved that case. I didn't have much make-up then, but what I did have I treasured.

I had a couple of cuddly toys that I still loved from when I was a baby, most especially Sad Bear, so named because I think he has the saddest-looking face ever! Grandad John bought him for me when I was small, so he was really special to me. He was propped up on my pillows with the other cuddlies. There was my silver TV and my VHS player in their usual places. My rings and bits of silver jewellery were hanging on the necklace stand. There were even a few copies of *Vogue* still kept there by Mum, in case I was ever able to come upstairs and read them. It was my private sanctuary, and I needed a moment to take it all in.

Laying me on the bed, Darren disappeared downstairs and I stayed up there a while, flat on my back with my head propped on the pillows, watching a few things on video. I texted Katie, who replied *Yay, you're home!!!!! xxxxx*, and all together, it made the sense of homecoming complete.

The day of my birthday finally dawned. The hairdresser came over in the morning to help get me ready; the party was planned for the afternoon, as I got too tired at night to go out.

Looking back, it seems like such a kid's party, but I was really excited, and insisted that the hairdresser straighten my hair. Then my carers helped me into a pair of jeans, even though they felt uncomfortable to sit down in. I didn't have any feeling in my skin or legs, but the weight and 'give' of whatever fabric I was wearing affected how I sat. Katie was the first to arrive, so that we could get ready together.

I had gratefully relinquished the Frankenstein chair once I could wheel myself around, and now had a (still horrible) purple NHS wheelchair. This one had a sheepskin backboard which helped to keep me upright and feel more supported.

All the activity and movement of the preparations, with people coming and going, and my nervous excitement, came together, plus I started to sweat heavily.

Because of the injury, I cannot regulate my body temperature, so when I'm hot I can't sweat to cool myself down and when I'm cold, my body cannot warm itself. If I sweat, it's AD kicking in. When I'm in pain or need the loo without realising, it's the autonomic dysreflexia that starts up, and it did then (probably as my injury was still quite new). It's a horrible cycle. Being flustered doesn't seem to help, and the sweating often makes me more anxious.

Basically my body starts sending signals to my brain that cannot get through, whereas my general temperature-regulation problem (which means I'm pretty much always cold now in the UK, even with my heating on full blast!) was part of the actual injury, rather than an accompanying condition like the AD. I usually get cold sweats, which isn't very pleasant.

'Aargh, Katie, help me sort my hair out, it's going frizzy – I've got the sweats again!'

'Hair emergency! Nee-nawww! Dr Katie to the rescue!' I giggled as Katie plugged in the straighteners. She knew how I liked it; she'd styled it for me in hospital several times.

When Katie had finished, she stepped back, her head on one side, appraising me.

'Jord, you look amazing!' she screamed, jumping up and down excitedly. 'Honestly, you look totally gorgeous. All the boys will be slavering over you.' I laughed. Katie always had the ability to make me forget my worries. Years later, when I look back at photographs taken that night, I still looked ill and frail, not gorgeous at all in my eyes, but Katie was doing her best to make me feel better.

'It's going to be so much fun, you'll love it. Loads of people have helped make it special for you. God, and if anyone deserves it, it's you. Come on, let's go and have a really good time.' Katie grinned at me, slicked on a last-minute touch of lipstick and pouted.

I grinned, knowing I was looking as good as I could in my situation. The hairdresser had also made up my face, as I was still learning how to make my twisted hands grip the various brushes needed for a complete look.

I hadn't given up. Far from it; but for the party I wanted to look good. I had asked the make-up lady to concentrate on the highlighting, to bring light to my face. I wanted to highlight my confidence and self-belief that day. I wanted my look to be pretty and uplifting.

'Come on, we'd better get going or your guests will think you've abandoned them,' Katie added.

'All right! Don't forget my make-up bag, and let's bring the straighteners as well. I don't want another hair incident!' Chuckling, we went out to the car and I was lifted inside.

The party, which was organised by a close family friend, Gaye, was held at South Wootton Village Hall, and about twenty people from different schools came. Gaye had ordered in loads of pizza, and there was lemonade and soft drinks.

As I arrived a great cheer went up: 'Happy Birthday, Jordan!'

'Oh my God, thanks, guys, you're amazing!' I could hardly speak, I was so moved. There were big signs saying Happy Birthday, and pink balloons festooning every corner.

'Hey, Jordan, good to see you!' yelled one kid from school.

'Yeah, Jordan, welcome home,' said Cara, coming up and giving me a cuddle.

'Did you know Craig Powell is coming to sing?' I shouted back. Craig was a local guy, a great singer, and it was really nice of him to come and perform for us. It really was like the old days, chatting with friends, watching them messing around, even dancing when Craig sang. I had always loved being out and socialising, going to house parties and discos. It was great to reconnect with that part of my life.

'Hey, Jordan, how's about that Snap Dance we talked

about, d'you wanna go?' A lad from school bellowed over at me above the music.

'Yeah, come on, let's all go, it'll be a good laugh,' shouted another.

A large group of us had being messaging about going to a Snap Dance, which was a club night for under eighteens with no alcohol but with proper DJs and decent music. I was desperate to go, but as people started leaving, I couldn't even find the strength to push myself to the door to say goodbye. I was exhausted, and it had just been a small party!

I was thrilled to be asked to go with my friends, but by now I felt tired and achy.

With a pang of regret, I said, 'Goodbye guys, have fun. See you a week today at school.' I watched my pals leave, but smiled as Katie slipped over.

'See ya later, Jordan,' shouted someone.

'Yeah, see you in school on Monday,' shouted Cara. I was too weary to reply.

All I wanted was to go home and get into bed. I didn't complain, though. I knew how much effort had gone into organising the party for me, and I didn't want to upset anyone by telling them how tired I was feeling.

'Come on, I'm dying to go home, Mum. Thanks for the party, Gaye – it was amazing.'

Katie pushed me out. She was staying at mine for a sleepover, so I wasn't missing out really.

Later, at home, Mum ran me a bath. Katie pulled her swimsuit out of her overnight bag.

'I'm coming in with you!' she laughed. I loved that about her; she was always unpredictable.

'Oh my God, that'll be hilarious,' I replied. 'Mum, we're going swimming.'

Looking at Mum's puzzled face made us both burst into fits of giggles.

'You two,' said Mum, 'you're as bad as each other!'

Things didn't feel that different. My mates were still around, my best friend Katie and I were having fun. Perhaps school would be a breeze.

Would I still be able to ignore my disability at school? To pretend that nothing had changed? I desperately hoped I could.

10

Blend

Proud to be Different!

'Loads of us don't fit in, and that's OK! Dare to be different.'

'Morning, gorgeous girl, wakey-wakey! It's your first day back at school, a big day for you.' Mum crept into my room, pulling the curtains open. Soft autumnal light filtered into the room.

'Urgh, it can't be morning already!' I muttered from under my duvet, covering my face with my left arm. Early mornings have never been my favourite time of the day!

'We've got a few minutes before your carer arrives, so I wanted to tell you how much I love you and how very proud I am of you, with everything you've been through, not just that you're courageous enough to go back to school today,' Mum started, sitting on the edge of my bed and rubbing my shoulder.

'Honestly, when I saw you in that hospital bed with that great ugly metal halo round your head and the sandbags weighting it down, I thought that was it. If I'm honest, I couldn't see how you'd ever recover. I thought you might lose your special light for good, but I was so wrong,' Mum added, looking at me from the corner of her eye.

'My special light?' I giggled. 'Don't be silly, Mum, I'm still in here, I always have been.

'I'm not sure how brave I feel today, though, Mum. It's a bit weird thinking of going back to school. I feel like I've been away forever,' I replied with an uncertain smile.

'What you have survived would defeat so many people, Jordan. I don't think I'd be able to stay as cheerful as you do if I was in your position; I think I'd want to strangle everyone with frustration!'

We were both laughing now.

'I want you to know how special you are, and how much we all admire you, and now I'm going to stop before I start to cry.'

'Don't cry, Mum, come on.' I peeped out from under my arm.

'And look, no one is forcing you to go in today, you know that, don't you? If it's too much, you can always try another time . . .' Mum's voice trailed off. I'm pretty sure she said that deliberately to spur me on. I pride myself on rising to challenges. Mum always called me headstrong – with the emphasis on strong!

I sighed.

'I want to go in and see everyone. I've missed my friends; weirdly, I've even missed the lessons, and I can't believe I'm saying that. I just want to be normal again. Why should things be any different to how they were before? I'm still the same person inside.'

Mum and I grinned at each other. At that moment we heard the front door open and Hayley, my carer, popped her head round my door.

'Knock, knock! Hey, Jordan, hey, Jane. Big day today,' she said.

'Yeah, yeah! I'm almost ready, almost,' I groaned into my arm, which I had placed back over my face. 'Just a few more minutes.'

Hayley laughed. 'Right then, I'll go and make your breakfast. Veggie bacon sandwich?'

'Yes please. Thanks, Hayley.'

I could hear Hayley whistling in the kitchen as she worked. I liked her a lot. She had long, thick brown hair and a pretty face. She was always upbeat and funny, so we got on really well. Hayley would arrive at 8 a.m. and get me up and dressed.

During the day she'd help me with simple tasks such as setting up the computer for me, passing me the things I needed and making lunch and drinks. She'd usually leave at 5 p.m.

The night carer would come in at around 9.30 p.m. so

that I could be twisted overnight every three hours, though we'd just booked Hayley as a night carer for one evening a week as well.

Mum took care of me in the time we had between day staff and night staff.

Ten minutes later the door opened, followed by Hayley carrying a tray of orange juice, tea and my sandwich.

She eased my bed up and put the tray on my table, wheeling it over to my bedside and over the bed, setting my things within reach.

When I'd finished, it was time to get me up and washed. At that point we were waiting for builders to finish putting in a shower room downstairs for me, so it still had to be a bed bath, which I thought was totally gross!

An hour later, I was sat in my chair dressed in my uniform of white shirt, green- , grey- and purple-striped tie and black trousers. I felt OK, not too uncomfortable wearing it, so that was a good start. Hayley placed my table in front of me, this time with my make-up bag and products arranged on it. I was still finding my way with applying them, though I'd made massive leaps forward, so I stuck to a 'nude' look with just foundation, mascara and brow definition.

Every time I looked in my mirror, I confronted the cosmetic effects of the crash. I have two prominent lines of scarring on and above my left eyebrow, from my temple to my brow. It was cut open by glass from the shattered back windscreen. When surgeons sewed up the wound at the Queen Elizabeth

Hospital in King's Lynn they left fragments of glass inside me which had to be reoperated on at Sheffield. The thin, silvery lines that I still have today show me how close I came to losing my eye. Another reason to be grateful.

I have scars all over my body, and they all tell a story. From the traces on my eyebrow; the scar on my hip where the surgeons took bone to graft onto my cracked neck; the mark in my hairline left from shards of glass; the dimples on my forehead above each eyebrow showing where the metal halo was inserted into my skull; the small, individual scars from having moles removed, which I'll tell you about later; to the great wound that runs down my spine from the top of the back of my neck. They are all part of me and my journey, and I never seek to hide them.

Even though we might be embarrassed by certain parts of our bodies, we need to learn to embrace these 'flaws'. Today I am body positive. It is incredibly empowering, and it is something we can all be.

My scars look beautiful to me. They remind me of how close I was to dying, and how much I have to be grateful for as a result.

The mirror also showed me how hunched up I was by the cramping muscles around my neck. I had to shift position every few seconds, trying to stretch them.

My hands were resting on the table, my fingers drawn into themselves. My eyes looked bright. I looked hopeful, excited even, to be rejoining my classmates, though I saw the worry there too.

My shoulder-length blonde hair had grown back well after it was shaved in places for the metal halo to be drilled into my skull, and my hair looked clean, though the colour was dull – it had gone a dirty blonde colour, which I really didn't like.

I looked again at the scars on my brow and gently touched them, feeling the lines and getting to know them. My eyes followed the movement of my poor, crunched-up hands as I traced the irregular shape of my brow, seeing where it tailed off too quickly, the hairs becoming sparse at the tail. A centimetre or so to the right and I would have lost my eye.

When I'd finished doing my face, we watched television for a while, my sister Eden and I, singing along to *Hannah Montana*, her new favourite show. Eden would often come and sit with me and we'd watch movies and sing along to the soundtracks. We were very similar in that way, loving performing and music.

After lunch, Mum drove me to school with Hayley, who was going to support me while I was there.

It was so strange being back. The smells and sights were the same. Kids were pushing through the crowded corridors, the bell rang for the next lesson, there were shouts and laughs as children jostled and threaded their way to class. To be honest, I felt quite overwhelmed. I'd expected it to feel familiar and safe, but instead I could feel myself start to panic as sweat broke out all over my body.

Cara met us in the corridor and walked alongside my wheelchair to the maths class I was attending (why was it always maths?!). Once inside, my chair wouldn't fit under a desk so I had to sit at the back of the class, making me feel a bit isolated again.

Five minutes into the lesson, a phone went off (strictly not allowed!). With a gulp I realised it was mine!

Everyone looked round at me as the teacher joked, 'Nothing has changed, eh, Jordan!' Everyone, including me, burst into laughter.

It didn't take much for me to work out that I was way behind. I hadn't a clue what the teacher was talking about. Maths was never my strong point – I've never been interested in it – and that, combined with the time I'd missed, meant I had fallen far behind the others. As the lesson progressed, I grew increasingly more anxious. I was sweating heavily, and terrified people would notice.

At the end of the session the bell rang again and literally everyone shot off to the next lesson, leaving me and Hayley alone in the classroom. It was quite awkward, navigating our way out past the chairs, which had been left out by pupils dashing off.

I suddenly felt rather alone. It also seemed to me that people weren't as friendly as I'd expected. Familiar faces waved and said 'hi', but no one really helped settle me back in and it was pretty much left to me and Hayley to get through the afternoon.

It is probably unfair of me to say that. The school had made an effort to raise money for me in my absence, and had welcomed me back, with the proviso that I wore a 'seat belt' in my chair for health and safety reasons. I could see it was necessary, I guess, but it didn't help me feel included.

It must have been strange for pupils to see me looking so different. I could hardly hide my chair or my injury, and I might have looked a bit frightening. It was obvious to them, and to me as well, that I didn't fit in any more. I was different, and that made me separate.

At the end of the day I arrived home exhausted, feeling as if my expectations both of myself and my friends had probably been quite high. I decided to go back again and spent two more afternoons at school over the next few weeks, but the same thing happened. On both occasions I ended up in the disabled loo having panic attacks.

I was still ill. It became obvious to me that things had changed. I wasn't the same as I was before the crash, and people treated me differently, however well meaning they were.

At that point I made the decision to stop going to school. I was still determined to go to college, however, and so I decided to be homeschooled. I would take my maths and English GCSEs the next year, and in the meantime I would choose to stay where I felt comfortable.

That decision was the start of my accepting that from then on I was always going to be someone who doesn't fit the mould, who simply doesn't fit in. I *was* different. I *wasn't* the same girl as the one who'd been at school at the start of Year Ten – and that was OK! Why would I want to be the kind of person who blends in, anyway?

From that moment, I decided to celebrate my differentness.

When I equate my findings to the process of applying make-up, I think of blending things together so that they work in harmony. I'd always need carers to harmonise and support my home life. They'd have to fit in, and we'd have to work together.

As in life, so it is in make-up. All the elements – foundation, concealer, blush – need to be blended together to achieve a flawless look.

Blending is one of the most important skills. It's all about the blending! To smooth over each layer, making them all work together, is an art form. Each layer has to be worked in properly to create graduation in tone and colour, rather than stripes or lines. After all, none of us wants to look like Neapolitan ice cream!

I use a stippling brush, which has lots of different fibres, with no powder or product on it, to blend everything that has been applied as a base. It works it all in together, softening the application and creating a natural sheen.

I use my foundation brush under my chin to prevent

tidemarks, making sure my neck and face match by blending the foundation down from my face onto my neck. I use it over my cheeks and forehead to blend down blush and then bronzer.

If only life, and particularly other people, could be worked together, creating harmony and not friction!

Blending is the way I finish the base of my look, before I work properly on my eyes and lips, so I know that the effect is flawless.

Blending eyeshadow is the most important area to work on properly. An eye can look dreadful if it's not blended properly – you can see some of my tutorials on YouTube which explain this in more depth. I can spend a long time blending out the darker shade in my eyelid crease. I make sure each eyeshadow I apply blends seamlessly into the other, to achieve a gradient effect.

Yet again, real life has often seemed to me to be a process of blending out disharmony, and perhaps that's why I love this part of my beauty routine so much.

The process of bringing things together, of smoothing over the lines and places that might be too dark or too light, is a way of balancing things out. I really enjoy that feeling, I guess because much of my life has been about sticking out, not fitting in.

It is a fact that some of us don't blend in. Some of us don't fit the mould. Perhaps that's something you understand too.

When I was bullied it was horrendous, but it also taught me how strong I am, how fearless. I kept going back into that school day after day in Year Nine, even though I was utterly excluded. I even watched as lines of girls turned their backs on me and walked through the gates together each morning. People can be cruel.

Yet I didn't crack. I didn't leave. I faced it down, and in the process I accepted that I'm one of those people that stand out, for whatever reason. There was something that marked me out as unusual; who knows what that was? But it gave me the perfect launching point for the work I do now. I didn't change who I was, either with the bullies or with my new situation as a wheelchair user. I stayed myself.

Looking back, I'm incredibly proud of myself for staying true to who I was; who I am. It has helped me find the strength to deal with my injury, as my disability took me to an even more extreme level of not fitting in. I've made my vlogs as a way of showing the world that I have something to offer, and whether you're interested in beauty or not, I hope the very fact that I have a passion in life, and have created my own successful career, can be a source of inspiration – especially to those who can relate to some or all of my struggles.

And look at how many people so far have watched my vlog, 'My Beautiful Struggle'! More than five million people have watched that on YouTube. On Facebook it's closer to seventeen million! Not bad for a quadriplegic! All those people connected with me enough to stop what they were doing and watch my video.

How amazing is that? I guess what I'm saying, both to myself and to you as you read this book, is that you may not fit in right where you are, but it doesn't mean that by being true to yourself and searching for the life you want to live, you won't find your tribe, your group, your soul people. I have. I've found my tribe online.

Obviously I have a small group of good friends around me as well. I have Mike, my fiancé (I'll tell you more about him later!), and my family, and my friends Katie and Kerrie (from uni) and Sam, Grace and Carley, to name a few.

I felt so strongly about this issue that I made a vlog called 'I Don't Fit In and That's OK', which is part of my series of motivational videos. I know a lot of my followers, you guys out there, feel, or have felt at some point in your lives, the same as me. You feel you don't fit in anywhere, just like I did.

People wouldn't talk to me at school for ages. Then, after my accident, people seemed scared to approach me. Even when I give talks these days (sometimes even at blogger events), people don't really come up afterwards, and I guess my being in a wheelchair is the thing that puts people off. Perhaps they're scared of it, or perhaps it makes them feel awkward. Either way, it can be an isolating experience for me.

And if you have anything that makes you stand out, not

necessarily a wheelchair but something about you that's a bit different, then the same thing can happen. But I think we have to celebrate our differences, because they make us who we are. I've made my disability a positive aspect of my life, when the temptation is to have only negative thoughts about it.

Just like with the bullies at school, I was determined to ignore my injury, in the sense that I could still make a successful life for myself, and I have, out of the sheer will not to give up, not to disappear like people in wheelchairs are sometimes expected to do.

These days, I think having good people around you is so important to your success. Being selective about people is a positive thing. I guess others may think my wheelchair is uncool, or even scary, but nowadays I don't care what people think. I'm determined to carry on being Jordan, with all that that entails. I make a point of not conforming to others' expectations of me. I don't try and fit in to be something I'm not – and you shouldn't either.

My persona on YouTube is exactly who I am in real life. I'll always say hello if you come and speak to me, just as I'll always reply in some way if you message me. I can get on with anyone, but I won't change myself for anybody, and if I have a message throughout this book, it's that.

You're unique. You're special. Celebrate who you are, just as I am doing, because only then will your tribe find you.

11

Toolkit

Facing Reality

'When something scares you, know that it could be the very
thing that could be your greatest accomplishment.'

'Will the defendant please stand up.'

The magistrate leant forward across her desk, her glasses
set firmly on her face. She looked stern. I knew that if I ever
had to face her I'd be a nervous wreck!

'Tell the court your name, please.'

This time it was me who leant towards the boy whose
actions changed my life forever. He stood in King's Lynn
Magistrates' Court in his dark, ill-fitting suit, his head
bowed, his voice barely a whisper.

He replied quietly. I could hardly hear him.

'And what do you plead?'

There was silence in the courtroom, the chatter from

the people who were crammed in behind us hushed as we waited to hear him, though I already knew that he had pleaded Not Guilty to the charge of Driving Without Due Care and Attention.

I expected him to deny it again, so when he muttered the word *guilty*, I couldn't believe my ears. I turned my chair an inch so I could meet Mum's eyes. They said the same as mine. Victory.

It was a year and a day since the accident; a strange anniversary. We'd spent a quiet day together, Mum, me and Eden, reflecting on the past twelve months and feeling trepidation about the forthcoming court case. That morning I'd woken up earlier than usual and lay in my bed, staring at the ceiling and wondering if going to hear the verdict would be as difficult as I imagined. Part of me was scared of seeing him, and I was nervous, too, at the effect it would have on me, whether I'd want to cry with frustration or shout with anger. I didn't want my hard-won peace of mind upset again, but at the same time I had to be there, I had no choice; and anyway, I wanted to hear what the magistrate was going to say. I also had the instinctive feeling that something about this day would bring a sense of closure.

Eventually my usual morning routine took over. Our family friend Jackie was looking after me that day, and she also straightened my hair for me. I was dressed in a smart pair of black trousers and a grey sheepskin gilet. I wanted to look my best, to hold my head up high in court and show

Tim that I was strong enough to live through what the accident had done to me.

We came to leave. I was flanked by members of my family: Mum was there, of course; my Nanno; Nanny Janice (my biological father's mother); Darren and his parents. Even though I had no contact with my dad, Mum and I had spent my childhood, every other Saturday afternoon that we weren't staying with Grandad John, with Nanny Janice. It sounds odd, but somehow it worked for us.

Neither Mum nor I had been bothered about my real dad disappearing from our lives, and we never saw him when we were at Nanny Janice's. I don't know where he was at that time, and I'm not even aware that I have had any face-to-face contact with my dad since I was a baby. If I had, then I'd forgotten it, but Nanny Janice was a part of my life, and it was great that she was also there to support me and Mum that day.

We drove to the court, and on arrival Mum and I were ushered into a side room. It was in there that I told the waiting police officer something that changed everything: the crucial piece of evidence that would change Tim's plea – and make sure that justice was done.

'Are you sure he said those words, Jordan?' The male police officer, who must have been in his mid-thirties, looked up at me quizzically.

'Yes, he definitely did,' I replied firmly. 'I was in shock when the police first came to take my statement; I can hardly remember them coming to the house. It was after leaving hospital that they spoke to me, as I guess I was too ill before then.

'I was really anxious about it, because quite a few months had passed since the crash and I was worried I would forget things. And I realise now I forgot the most important detail of all.'

The officer sat looking at me, his eyes searching mine.

'I think I blanked it out – making the statement, I mean. It was traumatic, reliving that day . . .' I looked down at my hands, then back up at him.

'To be honest, I don't know why I forgot,' I said, 'but I'm absolutely sure that's what Tim said.'

'Repeat it again to me,' answered the policeman, his pen hovering over the sheaf of papers holding my version of the events of that day, and my ten-page Victim Personal Statement containing details of those vital minutes and seconds before we swerved off the road.

I exhaled deeply. 'Tim said: "Let's lose them", when he saw the lads in the car behind, and that's when he sped up. Seconds later he was going way too fast, the car hit a large puddle, aquaplaned, and you know what happened next.'

The police officer looked at me again, then he seemed to make a decision. He got up quite abruptly and told us to stay where we were and wait a little longer. I didn't know it, but he went to speak to the magistrate – and presumably Tim and his representative.

The hearing began minutes later. When I heard Tim give his guilty plea, I was sitting at a desk in my chair directly opposite him. He did not look up once; he didn't catch my eye, or acknowledge my presence in any way. And it wasn't just him. His mother and girlfriend sat on the bench on either side of him, their eyes cast to the floor. I don't know if it was guilt, shame or perhaps even indifference that made them avoid my gaze. It was the first time I'd seen him since the crash, and it was the first time he would have seen me as well.

The magistrate postponed the case till after lunch in order to consider Tim's punishment. There was murmuring throughout the court. Tim and his girlfriend stood up and went outside, followed by his mum. I watched them go, relieved that he'd made the right plea.

My family and I decamped to sit in a nearby café eating sandwiches, drinking strong tea and talking, though the atmosphere was understandably muted. On returning to the courtroom, I remember staring over at Tim, coolly appraising him. He looked younger than his eighteen years, with his wet-look gelled hair which had been styled into spikes. I'd heard a few stories about him having a new car and showing it off to girls at parties during that last year, but they were as much gossip as fact and I tried to ignore them.

I had been scared of seeing him, as much for the emotions he would rouse in me as my fear of being in the same room as him. He looked scared, too, and I admit I thought he looked pathetic.

The magistrate had read my Witness Statement and the long Victim Personal Statement, and she said she was moved by it. As she spoke she glanced over at me, and I saw tears in her eyes. She was visibly affected by the impact of the crash on me and my family. Mum had had the chance to write her point of view in the statements as well.

The magistrate's voice hardened as she looked over the bench to stare at Tim, who was still looking at the floor.

He was sentenced to a driving ban for eighteen months, with 150 hours of community service. Tim was also ordered to pay £350 costs. It was at this point that he turned to his mother and sobbed in her arms.

My pity turned to disbelief – sobbing over a short driving ban, when I was paralysed for life! It hardly seemed possible. For a brief moment I wondered if perhaps he was crying from remorse, or from a sense of what he'd done, even though he didn't deliberately set out to harm me. But looking back, I don't think that was the case. I think he was crying for himself. I say that because he went on to appeal his sentence at Norwich Crown Court, an appeal which was dismissed on the 23 June 2006.

Suddenly I burst into floods of tears. The case was over. Tim was guilty and had his sentence. It was all too much. My hunched-up shoulders ached. I couldn't bear to be in that courtroom a second longer.

'Let's get you home,' Mum said, grabbing my wheelchair handles and turning me away from the sight of Tim weeping. I thought I was upset, but what I was really feeling was anger. My shock, my disbelief, every emotion I had felt until now turned into a form of pure rage. It's weird that I cried, but it was the only release I could manage. Even as the tears ran down my face, I knew this was the next phase of my recovery.

We didn't celebrate; it didn't feel right. Instead, we drove home and sat together drinking tea, hardly speaking. I couldn't get the image of Tim crying out of my head.

'We won, that's all that matters. You've got to let it go now, Jordan, and move on with your life. You can't change things and you can't go back,' said Mum softly.

I didn't reply. She was right. It was time to put the past behind me. We'd all had a difficult year; not just me. The trauma of the accident had affected everyone, but at the end of 2005, just over five months before, my beloved Grandad John, my mum Jane's dad, died at the age of seventy-two.

It hadn't been a shock. He'd been ill for a long time, and to the family it was felt just as much as a blessed relief that he was out of his suffering. By the time John had entered the Goodwins Hall nursing home in King's Lynn a few years earlier, he was already losing his memory.

After my accident I visited him twice, and neither time did he recognise me at all, staring blankly at my chair, his face showing confusion. I was glad that he didn't recognise me then. He'd have been deeply upset at the thought of his granddaughter being paralysed. It would have broken his heart.

I shed no tears at his funeral, even though I had so many happy memories of him. I tried to make Mum laugh by reminding her of how Grandad would dance to 'Jive Bunny', even though his balance was pretty awful, and how we were terrified he'd fall over while getting stitches from laughing so much, but Mum just nodded.

Perhaps I'd said goodbye to him a long time ago, but for Mum, of course, it was the death of her father, her dad, and she grieved deeply. I'd also lost the only real father I'd ever known. I was just so grateful I could be there to support Mum. It was my chance to give back after all the months she'd stayed with me in hospital.

Grandad died not long before Christmas 2005. It was our first Christmas since the crash, the first without Grandad, yet we were all determined to celebrate and be grateful for being together.

'Happy Christmas, sugar, you look super-glamorous today!' Mum commented brightly on my present, a bright pink Juicy Couture tracksuit, that I insisted on wearing straight away. She was putting a brave face on her grief.

'Thanks, Mum, you too. It's great to see you dressed up again.' I knew we were all holding ourselves together for the sake of each other. That's what you do when you love people.

I loved my new joggers. If I was going to have to wear casual, comfy clothes forever, then I'd make sure they were as trendy as possible!

'Happy Christmas, Mum. You too, Eden. You look so pretty in your new Christmas dress.' I beamed at my little sister, who was nearly five years old. She'd started school in September, and was growing up fast. She spun round, holding onto her red dress, thrilled to be the centre of attention.

'So, who's going to open the first present? Ah, I bet it's you, Eden.' I wheeled after her as she skipped into the living room where the tree stood. Mum had stacked the presents into piles, one for each person, just as I used to do every year. I don't know why I always did it; I do like things to look neat, though!

Eden shrieked with joy as she opened one Barbie after another. I smiled, remembering how happy I'd been receiving my first-ever Barbie doll. The expectation as I tore off the shiny paper. The joy at seeing the top of Barbie's blonde head as I unwrapped her. It seemed like a million years ago. I was so into girly things as a child; I refused to wear trousers and only wore dresses. I had been devastated on my first day at school when I discovered that the teachers assumed my name meant I was a boy. They'd put a picture of an aeroplane on my coat peg! I cried fat tears over that.

I'd adored Brownies, and stayed on a year longer than I was meant to as the Brownie leader hadn't the heart to chuck me out, and I would try out Nanny Janice's high-heeled shoes at the age of four, wobbling from side to side as I attempted to walk in them. Janice had small feet, so I felt they 'almost' fitted me, when in reality they were still miles too big!

I also had a special friend, Claire, who lived next door. I was besotted with her as she was a bit older than me, and I had memories of going into school and telling the teachers I had a big sister called Claire. They all knew I was, at that point, an only child! I'd been so desperate for a sister, I even drew pictures of 'my family' with Claire crayoned next to me! Then when Eden came along, I was so happy. She was the cheeky heart of our family.

My happy childhood laid the foundations of my life, giving me the right components in my emotional toolbox: resilience, positivity and an ability always to see the silver lining in any cloud.

I'd needed those attributes more than ever.

Life sometimes sucks, and there's nothing we can do about it but accept it and move on. Sometimes we need to reach deep within ourselves to find the courage to keep going.

It differs with everyone, but we all have an emotional toolbox, the skills and strengths we can use to overcome our challenges. Take a moment to work out what's in yours. Knowledge is power – and the point of life is to become empowered, to take charge of your own destiny and to become the best version of yourself you can be. I have learnt so much about myself, with everything I've gone through.

I know I'm kind, I have a big heart and I am fiercely loyal.

I've also discovered that I am able to face my fears, however uncomfortable it feels. It doesn't mean I'm not terrified, like I was before seeing Tim again – it just means I don't let that fear control my life and my decisions. Do you know the phrase 'feel the fear but do it anyway'? That has been the miracle behind my greatest areas of growth, my biggest successes.

As I write this I'm surrounded by more make-up products than I can count. I have an entire room that functions as my beauty toolbox! I have drawers filled with foundations and lipsticks, cupboards filled with products grouped together and pots of brushes. They are all special, all important parts of the looks I create, just as each part of our character is unique and special. The different products make up my toolbox, just as my different assets make up my character. They all have their place in dealing with what life throws at us.

It would have been so easy not to have gone into that courtroom, or hidden away as a quadriplegic young woman, too fearful to be herself again despite the injury. But I wouldn't let myself do that. I knew I was worth more, and so are you. You are worth so much. You just have to recognise it.

It isn't just 'bad' things that can make us more resilient. I think we can create our own destiny either way; be conscious about what we want to achieve and how we go about achieving it. My life is a testament to this desire, and yours can be too. What do you want? What parts of your character will you need to draw on to achieve it?

There is nothing stopping you from achieving your heart's desire, just as I choose to act as if nothing is stopping me.

12

Gloss

Making an Entrance

'Sometimes you have to "fake it to make it", especially on less-than-confident days!'

'Katie, you look even more paralysed than I do!' I cackled over at my best friend.

She was being held aloft in the arms of a male family friend who looked more like a Chippendale! His chest was bare and tanned. He had rippling muscles and was wearing a small black bow tie around his neck and a pair of black tuxedo trousers.

Katie screamed with delight, making the crowds that had gathered round our black Chrysler car cheer their approval.

'Woo-hoo, look at me, I'm doing all right, aren't I?' Katie crowed, waving to the crowds like she was the Queen!

I burst into laughter. Katie loved an audience, and most

of all she loved to have fun. Our friendship had grown steadily over the last months since I'd left hospital, and she was one of the main people I could rely on to be on my side – an ally, if you like.

'Whoop! My turn!' I shouted as I was lifted, more carefully this time, by the other bronzed man with bulging arm muscles and curly black hair. He was dressed – if you can call it that – the same as the other guy, in nothing but a black bow tie and a pair of smart tuxedo trousers. Both men looked like male models but they were, in fact, family friends who had offered to help us.

It was 18 May 2006, the court case was over and it was time to celebrate, to move on with my life, and in true Jordan form, I did it in style.

It was our school prom. I'd said from the start, even while lying in my hospital bed, that I was thinking of going. What sealed my decision was that the local newspaper, the *Lynn News*, had written a front-page article months earlier about my surviving the crash, saying I was vowing to go to the prom despite my injury.

It read:

INSPIRED BY PARALYSED JORDAN

A beautiful teenager is determined to go to her school prom despite being paralysed from the chest down after breaking her neck in a car accident . . . Mum

Jane Bone said: 'Jordan is slowly getting stronger through physiotherapy and is starting to use her arms and getting some feeling in her fingers.'

A reporter had spoken to Mum while I was in hospital, and she'd flippantly mentioned the prom, but we never expected them to make headlines of it! It left me with little choice. I *had* to go to the prom. I couldn't back down when apparently I'd made such a public statement! And so I decided that if I was going to go then I was going to make a proper entrance. I wanted to show everyone that my injury was no barrier to having a good time, or being glamorous.

So Mum, Katie and I had organised the car to take Katie and me to the school, right up to the entrance of the prom itself. We had been planning it for days. Inside the Chrysler with us would be the two men who would carry us out in front of everyone. Our car was decorated inside and out with pink balloons and a big pink bow at the front of the vehicle. There was no way we would be missed!

As I was held aloft, I saw the balloons being released into the mild spring air. They drifted over us, and I had a burst of pure joy. I grinned over at Katie as she waved back at me. Friends were calling to us, and we laughed in response, enjoying the party atmosphere.

We had both spent hours getting ready, and we knew we looked the business. Katie wore a pretty pink floor-length gown with a wrap, her hair perfectly straightened and full make-up. I was wearing a gorgeous turquoise-blue off-the-shoulder dress that had to be fitted to me as I was so slim. I'd made a special effort with my make-up, with the same blue colour worked into my eyes and a cool, shimmering pink lip to seal the look. Our neighbour did my hair, curling it then pinning it up so that strands of it fell around each side of my face.

Katie brandished a mirror when she'd finished.

'Look at you, Jordan Bone, you're a stunner!' I peered into the glass. My reflection smiled back at me. It was one of the first times since the accident that I felt I looked OK. I looked alive and happy! My hair was shiny at last, my make-up was pretty good. I felt radiant. Katie had looked me up and down, sitting in my prom dress with full make-up on, hair straightened and pinned up, and whistled a low sound.

'You look beautiful. You'll knock the socks off everyone in there tonight. There won't be a girl who looks better than you, I promise you. The boys won't know what to do with themselves.'

I laughed shyly. 'Don't be silly, you look gorgeous too. They won't keep their eyes off you either, Katie. Anyway, all anyone will see is my wheelchair, surely?' I felt tears dart suddenly behind my eyes. It was a big night for me; a defiant night. A night where I got to show myself off, and show the world that there was life even with paralysis. In some small way I felt I owed it to everyone out there who had had the kind of injury I had, and who perhaps felt ignored or excluded as a result. I know it was just a prom, but it meant so much to me. I'd got through the court case, and now I had a chance to get out there and enjoy myself, in my own way.

'So what if they see your wheelchair?' snorted Katie in response. 'If they're dumb enough to only see that, and not how gorge you look or how sweet and kind you are, then they're the disabled ones!'

I almost choked on my coffee as I was sipping it through my straw.

'That's so not PC!' I laughed. 'But who cares? You're right. My wheelchair is part of me now. It's like an extension of my body, my own personal accessory. If I don't celebrate it, then who will? Without it I'd be lost, totally dependent and probably lying down forever. I promise I won't ever be ashamed of my chair again. I might even dress it with balloons as well.'

'Don't you dare, you'll distract everyone from your gorgeousness.' Katie and I both burst into peals of laughter.

Despite the hilarity of getting ready with my mate, I was shaking with fear by the time the car drew up at our house. Katie squeezed my hand, though of course I could barely feel it. Some awareness had come back to my fingers over time, so they weren't totally lost to me, but I still couldn't move them, and probably won't ever be able to.

I hadn't said how I felt, but Katie only ever had to look at

171

me to know what was going through my mind.

'It'll be amazing,' she said softly, 'you'll see.'

'It's weird,' I replied, 'I suddenly feel nervous at seeing everyone. Some people at school I haven't even seen for months. What will I say to them? D'you think they'll even bother to talk to me?' I asked, feeling a bit downcast. Not everyone I'd been friends with before the accident had stayed in touch, and that had hurt. Obviously I had really close friends I could rely on, but even so, I had felt a little rejected, but I also knew I could perhaps be a touch over-sensitive when it came to friendships. They were so much a part of me that I felt any slight – real or imagined – keenly.

'Anyone who doesn't speak to you isn't worth the bother! Your true friends will be there. Me, Cara, Kirsty, Amy and Catherine are going. We'll all be chatting so much you won't notice whether anyone else hangs out with us or not,' Katie answered cheerily, naming some of the girls I'd become close to recently.

She looked so sincere, I immediately cheered up.

'Sorry, didn't mean to put a downer on things. It'll be fantastic. Look, I'm super-happy again! Let's go and have fun!'

'Yay, that's the Jordan I know and love. Come on, let's rock this prom night!'

Katie grabbed my wheelchair handles and steered me outside to the waiting car.

*

It was no wonder I was anxious about going. I hadn't been back since my fairly disastrous attempts to go to class. I'd been homeschooled in maths by a sweet elderly man. He was quite short with white hair and rosy cheeks. I'd embarrassed myself once by falling asleep during a particularly demanding session. That day I was sitting in a comfy leather recliner at home rather than in my wheelchair. I still had bouts of tiredness, and also I didn't sleep for long periods at night because of having to be rolled, so I dozed off, then woke myself with a small start.

None of the lessons did me much good. When it came to the GCSE I'd insisted on writing it myself, but it was still fairly illegible and so my multiple choice answers were probably difficult to read. It was no surprise to me that I failed it! But hey, I'd never planned on being a maths genius anyway!

In the evenings I also had an English teacher, a tall, well-spoken man with a mass of dark hair which was going grey. I'd always loved English, so those sessions went much better and I ended up passing my GCSE, which made me really happy. Some of my friendships had tailed off during this time between ending school and going to the prom. I understood that people's lives moved on; they got new girlfriends or boyfriends, hung out with different crowds, and of course, I couldn't just come along and hang out in the park or shopping centre any more, as I needed a carer with me when I was out.

I knew that those things presented difficulties at exactly the time teenagers want to go out and be carefree. It was a shame, though, to lose contact. I guess that was another reason I wanted to make a splash at the prom – to show people I was still me and could still have a good time.

Mum had driven over to school earlier so that my wheelchair was waiting for me when we got there.

There were no ramps up to the hall entrance, which is why I'd elected to be carried, though it had been a surprise when Katie demanded that she was carried as well. Trust her to make me feel at ease, to show solidarity when I was nervous. Being carried in was also a million times more glamorous than being pushed round to the disabled entrance at the back of the building!

The evening itself was not as cool as we'd hoped. The school hall still looked like the school hall, with our rows of dining tables and chairs, a few decorations livening it up a bit. There was no DJ, just a sound system, but people did get up and dance so it wasn't too bad.

Katie wheeled me to the end of the tables nearest the disabled loo. Cara, Catherine, Amy and Kirsty joined us for most of the evening, eating at the table together before they too went off to dance. Katie stayed with me, even though I knew she loved to get up and show off her moves. At that point, I was too weak and unconfident to boogie.

'Go on, Katie, go and have a dance. You know you want to.' I sipped my fizzy drink through a straw and indicated with my hand that she should go and join the others.

'No way, Jord! I'm not leaving you sat here by yourself. We can watch everyone and have a laugh instead!'

I looked over at the crowd. There seemed to be an invisible line around my chair that prevented people from coming up and saying hello. I said 'hi' a few times to old friends and they waved and smiled, but didn't approach.

By the time the night came to an end I was weary to the bone and feeling upset, probably as much out of tiredness as the sense that I was 'off limits' nowadays.

'They don't understand, Jord. How can they? You look the same, but you're not the same as them any more. You've been through a massive life experience, and those people who ignored you tonight can never connect with that. Please don't take it to heart.'

I knew Katie was being kind to spare my feelings, but it was obvious that people had moved on and found other friends.

When we arrived, all eyes were on us. It was entertaining and exciting. Now I felt the eyes were still on me, staring at me, but in a different way, in a way that made me separate from them.

I sighed. 'I know I expect too much from people. I haven't even been at school for six months; why would they hang out with me?'

Suddenly the evening felt like a failure, my hopes bursting like the balloons. My sheen faded, and by the time Katie and I arrived back at mine I felt genuinely upset. I saw that I had created a superficial lustre for the prom. But I didn't regret it, however painful it felt then.

I learnt not to hide my disability away, but I also learnt a powerful lesson: that standing out isn't always easy. I could see this was something I would have to accept about my life, and master.

Katie stayed for a sleepover. We lay chatting for ages, mulling over the night.

'I'm going to apply for college. I've made up my mind,' I stated, staring up at the black of the ceiling.

'Sounds good,' Katie yawned. 'You'll sock it to them.'

'There's nothing holding me back now. I've been carried in the arms of a man wearing only a bow tie and trousers through crowds of people. I am not invisible, and I'm going to just go for it from now on. I'm going to get out there, pushing through whatever barriers face me. I'm going to be a success, Katie, you just watch me.'

Katie's snuffled snores greeted me. I smiled into the darkness.

I'd survived another tricky experience, a night of being the main attraction in both good and bad ways, and if I'm OK with that, then there's nothing stopping me fulfilling my dreams.

I always try to make the best of what I have. It is like a philosophy. It means there is always a way of seeing past difficulties; a way of shining brightly, whatever the situation.

Sometimes we have to gloss over things. I felt like an outsider at the prom because I was wheelchair-bound. Yet I was determined to go and enjoy it to the very best of my ability. I made the most of what I had, and that's the starting point for anyone, regardless of where you live, who you are and what you've done. We can't change the cards we've been dealt, but we can learn to play them.

I would love to have gone back in time and never stepped inside that car driven by Tim, but that was wishful, pointless thinking. Instead I worked with what I had. I glossed over the fact that I hadn't been at school for a while and was unsure of the reception I'd get. I glossed over my disability and wheelchair by making sure I looked as good as I could. I made the night my own. I went on my own terms.

Slicking on that pink-coloured gloss was the final part of my make-up routine that day. It was the seal on my promise to go as Jordan, rather than as a paralysed girl.

My lip gloss helped me put a shiny front on things, ramping up the glamour and adding the finishing touch to all my efforts. I wouldn't have dreamt of going without it. I needed as much moral support as physical help that night, and my make-up provided part of that feeling.

As I've said, I believe there is a link between looking good and feeling good. Taking time with your appearance is a form of self-care. And it's also all about learning what gives you that thrill, that shiver of happiness, whether it's applying a lip gloss or dabbing paint onto a canvas.

I had to draw on my reserves of courage that night, and I'm so glad I did. I vowed to go to college as a result, and three years later I finished at King's Lynn College with an A level in Media Studies and a BTech in Journalism. I had managed to study, despite not being able to write by myself.

It wasn't the only bit of turbulence during that time, either. My mum and Darren split up while I was at college, so my family moved house. After that, my mum met her partner Michael. He's now such a father figure to me – always there for me and Eden – and he helped with the build of our new house. I can't express how grateful I am to him; we wouldn't even be living where we are if it wasn't for Michael's hard work. So sometimes change is good!

I realised that I had managed to stare back boldly at those who couldn't help but look at me, checking out the blonde in the chair! It was hard work. I'd needed a scribe and carers to help me while I was in college, though I had done a lot on my laptop.

But I'd done it.

To celebrate going to college, I took a month-long break in 2008, going on holiday without Mum, which was so brave of me! I went to Tenerife with a carer who had become a pal and her mum. It was a taste of the freedom I yearned for, with nights out having fun in the bars and clubs of Playa de las Americas. I got back exhausted, happy, but with a couple of bedsores, which meant I had to lie low for a few weeks.

Finishing college gave me a real confidence boost. It was then that I decided to *really* go for it.

'Mum, I want to go to university. I've made up my mind; it's what I want to do. I want to study fashion journalism, and one of my college teachers, Kay (who taught media studies) is going to help me. She's writing in support of my application. It's a long shot with only one GCSE, one A level and a BTech to my name, so I'm not massively hopeful of winning a place, but I'm going to try.'

Mum looked up from the computer. We were sitting in her study, both sipping mugs of tea. She turned to me and with a wide grin said: 'If anyone can do it, it's you, sugar. You go, girl.'

And I did.

13

Eyes

Looking Forward

'Acceptance is hard, but ultimately it changes everything. You *can* accept. You *can* move forward. You *can* succeed.'

Depression came from nowhere, or that's how it seemed. Perhaps in reality the seed had been planted far earlier, in the aftermath of the crash. Perhaps it had been creeping at my heels for a few years, since just after the court case. Whatever and however it arose, it seemed to sink into my bones, dragging me into a period of darkness.

I had achieved so much after my accident. I'd fought my way back from the brink of death. I'd learnt how to cope with almost complete paralysis. I'd gone to the prom, been to college, seen the driver of that car brought to justice and I'd even sat some exams.

Then, out of nowhere, it hit me.

Looking at it now, I can see that it was the point at which the reality of my condition, and the enormous effect it had on my trying to live my life, truly came home to me. Depression is never easy. It is bleak. It robs the life force, the essential spirit of a person, but even as I went into it I knew that it was about more than just feeling low. It was the start of my process of acceptance. It was painful, acutely so at times, but it was an essential part of my journey.

Suddenly all my ambitions and ideas vanished and were replaced by one phrase that went round and round my head: *What's the point?*

What's the point of doing anything? Of trying anything? Of living . . .?

I had returned from my holiday to Tenerife suffering from those annoying bedsores, which meant I had to spend a period of time lying down. That was the moment when the dark thoughts crept back into my mind. That was the time I felt hopeless and helpless, feeble and abandoned by the universe. My positive thinking dissolved into the darkness, not disappearing completely but smothered as if by smoke. I stopped texting friends. I spent more and more time alone, in my room, waiting for the low mood to pass.

Except it didn't; it got worse and worse until one day I simply didn't want to get up. My sense of humour and my chattiness seemed to vanish, leaving me feeling flat, bottoming out emotionally and experiencing a sense of complete isolation, despite my family, friends and carers who surrounded me.

It was the moment at which all my efforts to rebuild my life and move forward with cheerful purpose suddenly exhausted me. I felt disconnected from who I was, from my personality and character. One incident that showed me how low I'd become was when the cat brought a mouse into the house and deposited it in my carer's shoe. Everyone was cracking up, and I knew that normally I'd find it as funny as they all did. But that day all I said was, 'Oh, right.' Then I wheeled myself off to my room, realising that something was very wrong with me. I didn't feel human.

Later that day, I confessed to Mum how I felt.

'Mum, I don't want to live any more,' I said, matter-of-factly. Mum froze, turned to look at me for a second, then replied, 'That's it. I'm making you a doctor's appointment today. This needs to be sorted.'

I guess she'd noticed that I hadn't been myself in the weeks beforehand, but when I said what I said it was obvious that it wasn't a passing phase, or being 'a bit down'. I was depressed. It was a relief to admit it.

It was a dark time for me, and one I know thousands of people can relate to. At the time it felt like things couldn't possibly get better. I saw myself as I was: a quadriplegic, dependent on others for the rest of my life. I saw my struggles, and how they would never end. I would always have to make the best of things. I spiralled down into unhappiness, a place that felt hollow, bottomless. Nothing could make me smile.

The doctor prescribed me antidepressants. I was reluctant to take them initially, but he told me I wouldn't be hesitant if I was a diabetic taking insulin, or medication for some other sickness. He told me that mental illness was like having any other condition, except that it was the mind and not the body that was suffering.

It could be treated, with medication and counselling. Seeing it in that light, I understood that the taboos around mental health were nonsense. There must be thousands, if not millions of people out there who knew how it felt to be depressed, to feel that life wasn't worth living. Who was I to turn down appropriate treatment?

In January 2009 I began taking antidepressants and very gradually I began to feel more like my old self. Once I started taking the medication, I could feel the deep sadness and lack of interest for life lift. It wasn't that I suddenly felt completely happy, but it definitely took the edge off. I just felt that I could function on a basic level more easily. It was like the medication numbed the feeling of wanting to die and gave me a little boost, helping me to feel slightly more normal.

'You look at it, I can't read it,' I said to Mum as she held out the opened letter to me. The paper was white and crisp. It was folded neatly, and stamped with the logo of the University for the Creative Arts in Epsom, Surrey.

With my college teacher Kay's help I'd applied for the fashion journalism course. My hopes and dreams seemed to hang on this moment. Could a quadriplegic really go to uni? Could I really follow my goal of becoming a fashion journalist?

Looking at the letter, I felt overwhelmed with the sheer audaciousness of my application – and I was utterly convinced it held only rejection.

'All right, sugar, if you're sure. Here goes . . .' Mum's hands shook slightly as she unfolded it, her eyes darting quickly over the typeface.

'Aargh, don't keep me waiting!' I groaned. 'Tell me the bad news – I haven't got in, have I? I knew it. I knew it was a long shot; why did I think I could possibly get in? I'm a total idiot!' It had been a very long shot indeed, and one I was clearly desperate to believe would pay off.

'You silly girl! You got in, of course you did! Why would they refuse my beautiful daughter, eh?' Mum jumped up, waving the letter and whooping with joy.

'Jordan, you gorgeous girl, you've done it!' My head was spinning. I couldn't believe what I was hearing. 'Let me look, I need to see for myself.'

Mum flourished the document. 'It's all there in black and white, my lovely. You're going to uni!'

'Wow, that's so awesome. I did it, Mum. I really did it.' I

reread the letter, checking I'd heard right. I still didn't believe it, even though it was there on the page: *We are delighted to inform you . . .*

'Right, well, we need to think about this. It's going to take some organising, Jordan. You'll need to get down there early to settle in, and you might need to hire some new carers from the area. Gosh, Surrey, it feels so far away.'

For the first time, Mum looked worried.

'And it's not been easy for you recently, Jordan. Are you sure you're up to this? It's a big move.'

Mum was referring to my depression, of course. I wasn't entirely back to 'normal', but the antidepressants had helped me get back on track enough to be considering leaving home by myself for uni.

'Jordan, I don't want to overdo it, but this is, it's . . . I don't know how to say this, but going to uni is a move of, well, a move of breathtaking ambition.' Mum peered at me, her face a mixture of worry and pride in me. Things that were normal and straightforward to others were huge challenges for me, and going to university by myself would count as one of the most ambitious things I'd done.

Was I ready? Could I handle being away from those who cared for me, who loved me?

There was only one way to find out.

I was leaving the safety and security of home, where my needs were understood and met, to branch out on my own. Yet I was resolute. I was going. No one was going to stop me!

Arrangements were swiftly made, and in September I moved to Epsom, though the day I went, I was putting on my mascara and I dropped the wand. It was quite rare by then for me to do that, as I was getting really good at holding brushes. The applicator, coated in thick black mascara, fell onto my new white top. I burst into tears. I was still quite fragile emotionally.

Regardless, I carried on with my plans. I spent a week interviewing carers and found a nice lady to be one of my night staff, alongside the night carer I had in King's Lynn, called Lynne, who had agreed to come with me. My friend Amy was working for me by then, and so she came with me to be one of my day carers.

Amy stayed with me for a couple of months and then she left, so I had Becky and Angie for the rest of the time I was there.

At uni, I made amazing leaps forward in reclaiming my independence. The university itself was brilliant. They knocked two rooms together in the halls of residence so I could live alongside the other students, and they gave me a room for Lynne to use to sleep in during the day. Lynne became a mother figure while I was at uni; she truly cared for me, and I was so glad that I had her there with me.

When Amy was there, she was with me during the day and slept there overnight. So I wasn't short of good people around me.

I even managed to join in Freshers' Week, where the new intake of students have a sociable week, going to clubs and bars and making friends. It was brilliant having Amy with me, as she was my friend but she knew my needs too; it made it easy to go out with her, and we always had a lot of fun. Most of the social nights were in the Wetherspoons pub or in the club, the Boogie Lounge.

A girl called Kerrie moved into the room opposite mine. She had long brown hair and a kind face. Kerrie was only seventeen but had started uni because she was from Ireland and they go earlier over there. We always used to bump into each other in our hall kitchen, but we didn't speak much at first as I was always with Amy, but one day we decided to go to Harvey Nichols in London.

Unfortunately the trip turned into a bit of a weird experience. My carer that day, Angie, had to leave, and I allowed myself a couple of small glasses of wine. Then I almost passed out; I didn't know where I was. Kerrie was amazing. At the train station I made Kerrie lie me on the floor – I thought I was in a hotel room, and was chatting away to our friend who wasn't even there!

To this day I don't know why the alcohol affected me so badly; perhaps it was the medication, or perhaps my drink was spiked. Who knows? It's funny now, but at the time it was horrible. Kerrie managed to get me back to Epsom on her own. She looked after me brilliantly, and after that we became firm friends.

Classes were held in the main lecture hall. My carer was my scribe, while I sat at the front and listened. I'd be lying if I said it wasn't a struggle. The workload was pretty intense, and I had to work extra hard to keep up, especially as I would type up everything and do my assignments myself on my own laptop. I didn't want to be treated differently because of my disability. I never have, but looking back, maybe I could've been a little easier on myself and asked for more help at the time. Kerrie also loved fashion, and we were on the same course, so we worked together on some assignments, but I mostly did everything myself. It was pretty tiring.

One day I was feeling particularly shattered, so I was lying on my bed browsing on YouTube. I stumbled across a guided meditation, and I thought *why not?* That moment lit a spark in me that has never gone out.

I actually felt like the universe was giving me a helping hand. Perhaps it was also the time when I fell in love with the online community, and realised its incredible potential to spread positivity and inspiration.

I decided to try it out. The results were life-altering. The videos I found helped me to realise that we all deserve an awesome life, no matter what; it's just up to each of us to create that life. It might sound a bit obvious and clichéd, but by intently focusing on this idea, I truly believe it enables great things. You need to consciously remind yourself of your potential.

Lying back, listening to the uplifting mantras, I thought of the songs I had sung to keep my soul and spirit together. The lyrics had meant so much to me at difficult times, and this was the evolution of that need for guidance and positivity.

I gradually learnt to live in the moment. My mindset altered. I noticed that if someone did something that annoyed me, I didn't get cross, instead I wondered what had happened to them to make them act that way. I became more sympathetic towards people, more understanding and tolerant. That sense of tolerance also extended to myself. I knew deep down I'd been battling against my own demons: my anger at being paralysed, my regrets for the life I'd wanted to live but couldn't.

That was the first time I stopped fighting. I acknowledged.

The effects started to take hold. My depression gradually lifted. I felt like a phoenix rising from the flames, and I also found a whole new community of kind, interesting people online. I started following other positive thinkers, or meditation teachers, and I soon became part of this movement of positivity. It was then that I realised I could be one of them by making my *own* YouTube video.

After all, it was something else I could control completely by myself. I could set up my laptop, shoot a video using the webcam and edit it myself, then upload it to the channel. It was like dawn breaking. A new world suddenly opened up to me. I could see opportunities that I didn't have to struggle for. My vision of myself and what I could become expanded.

The twentieth of May 2010 was the first time I dared to speak out online. It was so nerve-racking! I set up my laptop by my window, relaxing music playing in the background, and I considered for a moment what to say. As I sat there the room suddenly filled with sunshine, creating a beautiful bright space, and I knew that was my cue to begin.

'Hi, everyone, hope you've all had a lovely day. I've been in university for most of it. I kind of thought, "Oh, there's going to be a storm," but storms are cool anyway.

'When I finished my class the sun was really shining and I thought, "Yes! I can go and do something now," so I went to the top of Epsom Downs – it's just beautiful. It's all countryside, but you can see London as well. It's bizarre but really cool. I thought, "Um, I want to explore a bit and find some more fabulous places." I got in the car and went up this huge, gigantic hill. It was huge, my ears popped!

'It was just so beautiful – it looked like something out of a movie. It just occurs to me that whenever the sun shines it releases all this happy energy. I believe it's a fact, as everyone I know says, "Yes, we can do this, we can do that" . . . You can do anything. You can have no money at all and still have a fantastic day sitting in the sun.

'Tomorrow I'm in university again and that kinda sucks

. . . I get really excited when it's sunny. I hope you have had a lovely day and have enjoyed the sun as much as I have. Peace and love.'

I blew a self-conscious kiss at the end.

My first-ever vlog.

I called it 'Super Sunshine', and to date it's been viewed nearly eighteen thousand times. Who could have known that that little broadcast, shot in my student room, would be the start of everything?

I didn't know it, but I'd begun to follow my heart, to open my eyes to the world and its opportunities. I started believing in what I *could* do, and I wanted to share that knowledge with others who might be struggling. It was like a breath of fresh air for me.

There was nothing fancy about my first vlogs. I shot them in daylight mostly, using my laptop and webcam. I didn't buy a proper video camera until much later. Once I started, I got the taste for it. I found myself blanking out in lessons, thinking of what I would say in my next video. I realised that as hardly anyone had seen them yet, I needed to tell people who I was and what had happened to me.

So I shot a vlog called 'Who is Jordan Bone?'. In it, I say 'Who is this girl? Who is this alien?' I was still searching for my true self, and I was content to share that journey with like-minded viewers.

'My name is Jordan. I'm twenty years old. I'm Scorpio, and I've been through so much in my life. When I was fifteen

I had a car accident and I broke my neck, and I'm a wheelchair user (I pushed myself around the room to prove the point!).

'That night completely changed my life. One minute I was a normal girl having fun with her friends, the next minute I was in hospital, like, what has happened to me?

'I knew straight away (about my paralysis). That's the thing; I became spiritually enlightened but it's only now that I'm kind of realising it, if that makes any sense . . .

'The car crashed, obviously, and it landed in a ditch upside down. I just remember not being able to breathe, hardly – well I couldn't, I had the seat belt wrapped around my neck, and, *oh my goodness I'm gonna die*. I just felt it, and I could see all this light, it was bright, completely white like the purest colour ever. I saw it and thought, *no, I'm not going, you can't get rid of me that easily, I've got so much to do* . . . I started singing "You've Got The Love To See Me Through". (I sing this line in the video!)

'And miraculously, I'm here. I believe now that I had an out-of-body experience; I felt like an onlooker, like I was watching a movie, looking down at what was happening. It was so strange. That will never leave my soul, that that experience happened.'

I feel a bit cringey about those videos now, as I see I was trying a little too hard to be positive and mellow. I called myself a Lightworker, and that's my way of acknowledging the thing that happened to me, and how being positive had got me through.

I also talked about one of my (many!) tattoos, one on my right forearm. I love tattoos, and mine all have meaning for me. In that video I go on to say: 'My tattoo is a key with a lock: the key is the lock with a rose in the middle. It can never be undone, and although it doesn't work it's still beautiful, which is how I try and represent myself. Even though I'm broken I can still be beautiful.'

My message was clear, even back then. It is the broken parts of me, body and soul, that are the most special. There's a saying about a cracked pot. It leaks water along the road and the owner of it looks down and sees that flowers have grown in the watered areas. I love that idea. I am a cracked pot. I will never be fixed, but perhaps my vlogs are like that line of flowers, little points of light showing people that you can be whoever you want to be.

After a year I left university, as I decided that my happiness was the most important thing. I'd been through too much to suffer being miserable. I was struggling with the coursework, and it started making me feel down again, so I followed my heart and it led back home, a move I have never regretted.

It is not always easy to follow our hearts. Meditation helped me to understand myself and what is best for me. It gave me the vision and focus to see further, to look at possibilities and situations with a wider perspective. It showed me there are always ways to help yourself in any given situation, and that is so empowering. It can work for you too, I promise!

I started concentrating all my time and energy on make-up, learning new skills to complement what I already knew. When applying eye make-up, shadows are as important as highlights in creating a balanced, flawless look. Through my depression and leaving home for uni, I'd experienced life in the shadows again, times of darkness punctuated by momentary spots of light. Those times, difficult as they were, enriched my recovery. The depression was visible proof that I was finally accepting things at a deep level.

And that, of course, is when everything changed – for the better.

Where there is darkness, there is also light. It is the same in life, no matter what hardships we face – even in the darkest times, there is always a light shining brighter.

In make-up terms, shadowing is a vital part of creating the look you want. I use dark eyeshadow to create hollows and dips, areas that recede. It is part of the trickery, or the magic, if you prefer, of beauty.

Today I use foundation as the base for my eyeshadow rather than eyelid primer. I build up colours, layering darker shades on top of lighter ones. I love a warm smoky eye.

I start off with a golden colour, using a fluffy brush at

the top of my eyelid crease, and circular motions to blend it in. Then I build things up with a darker shade in the same place, adding warmer tones through the crease using the same brush, which means everything merges together. With a smaller brush, which I position using my teeth, I add a pop of red on the outer corner of my lid and run that through the crease as well.

Then I blend everything using a clean brush. With a flat brush, I coat my eyelid with a gold shade to add glamour, then use a lighter, shimmery shade at the inner corner of my eye nearest each side of my nose. This makes my eyes appear brighter. I look fresher and more awake, and it also makes my eyes look bigger. I put a bit more red at the outer corner, running it under my eye as well, and some burnt orange on the lower lash line. I don't change my brush, so again, it is the combined effect of the colours that is so stunning.

Liquid eyeliner was probably the hardest product to relearn how to apply. It took all my ingenuity, using my mouth to get the top off, tensing my neck muscles as I strained to keep my hands steady and move them, and holding my head to the side to create a slick wing. So hard! Applying the liner always feels like a workout for me, because I have to tense my arm and neck muscles to keep still enough to get a straight, sharp line.

If any product proved to me that I could do anything I set my mind to, it was that one, because applying it was the trickiest to relearn. It showed me the best is always to come.

It reminds me I am looking forward, opening my eyes to every possibility. I have finally, truly accepted my fate, and my life is fully committed to my future.

In 2009 I'd had a tattoo on my left shoulder, a quote from a Lady Gaga song. Later that year, I'd met Lady Gaga at HMV in Oxford Street. She came up to me, saying, 'Hey, pretty lady, I love your disco pants!' as I was wearing sequinned leggings. Earlier that day I'd been in Topshop with Amy, and I'd bought two fake gold rings with the word LOVE as the design, one for me and one for Lady Gaga herself. I expected her to throw it away (especially as, within a day, the ring left green marks on my finger, it was so cheap!), but a week later, I saw her on TV at the Video Music Awards in America and she was wearing the ring I gave her!

I showed the megastar my tattoo, and she scribed the words on the back of my wheelchair, signing it with a flourish. What did my tattoo, and the quote on my chair, say?

She dried her eyes, picked up her microphone . . .

To me, those words summed up everything: my attitude, my resilience, my spirit.

14

Bronzer

Shocking News

'You have one life – don't waste it on regrets or fears,
go out and live it.'

'I'm sorry, Jordan, but it's bad news. The mole is cancerous. You have malignant melanoma.' The doctor paused, her voice sounding strangely distant at the end of the phone line. For the second time in my twenty years, I saw my life flash in front of me.

'Excuse me, sorry; I drifted off a bit. I'm feeling a bit spacey today,' I said. I may even have giggled. I guess it was the shock.

'OK, Jordan, no problem. Look, we'll need to book you in for another appointment urgently. We'll need to remove some more of the skin around your knee to check whether it has spread or not. In the meantime, it goes without saying – stay off the sunbeds.'

'Yes, OK, of course, doctor,' I muttered, still unable to put a coherent sentence together. 'It's good we've caught it early,' I added, before saying goodbye and ringing off. Mum was out, the house was empty as my carers were mostly in Epsom (I was still at uni then), and I was back home for the holidays. For a moment I thought about ringing Mum's phone to let her know the news, but I hesitated. I didn't want to spoil her day at work, so I hummed to myself as I wheeled back to my room to finish my meditation. It was a beautiful one that day, all about nature and how it makes us feel serene.

'Oh, well,' was all I said to myself.

Hours later, I heard the sound of Mum's key in the lock.

'Hello!' she shouted out to me. I wheeled out to greet her. She looked OK, a bit flustered maybe, but she'd just got in, and Eden ran past her and out into the garden. I waited till she was settled and we were in the kitchen, the light streaming into the room. Mum had her back to me, rummaging in a cupboard, when I broke the news.

'OK, Mum, don't freak out, but there's something I need to tell you,' I started.

Mum swivelled round.

'What do you mean, don't freak out? Oh God, what has happened, Jordan? Tell me quickly!'

'OK.' I breathed out. 'There's no easy way to say this, so I'll just come out with it. The results came back and I have a malignant melanoma. It's skin cancer, but they think we've caught it early. I have to go back to the doctor's to get more tests.'

I remember Mum's face. She looked dumbstruck.

'You've got cancer . . .'

'Skin cancer, Mum. The mole on my knee was dodgy. I've got to go back and get the skin removed. It's no big deal,' I said.

'It's no big deal!' Mum echoed, staring at me. I giggled. I couldn't help it; she looked so silly, like a fish caught on a riverbank, gulping for air.

'Honestly, Mum, it's fine. Whatever happens, it'll be OK whether there's more cancer or not.'

'What has happened to you? Are you on drugs? Why are you so, so . . . calm?' Mum practically shrieked.

She was right. I wasn't panicking. I knew I didn't even look that bothered by the news. Mum must have thought I'd gone into some kind of trauma, but after my initial reaction on the phone I'd steadied myself emotionally and had clicked into my positive-thinking vibe.

'Mum, the doctor said we shouldn't worry. It'll be fine, whatever happens. Honestly, Mum, it's OK. We can sort it out.'

'But, Jordan, it's cancer. It's bloody cancer, and it's not every day you hear that. I don't get why you're so relaxed about it.'

Mum looked really upset, and I could see she was more

stunned by the news than I was. Luckily the phone had rung when I was almost at the end of my online meditation, so I was in a good space inside myself.

Nothing else had changed that much in my life except that I was enjoying making my videos, and I was spending time going out with friends, but I was feeling better in myself, stronger, more able to cope. I wasn't fighting my injury any longer, and so I wouldn't fight the cancer diagnosis either.

I'd been visiting a local tanning salon for nearly five years, since sustaining my injuries, because it helped warm up my aching muscles and destressed me. I felt the cold badly since the crash, as I couldn't regulate my body temperature, and the heat of the tanning booth was a pick-me-up. I have always loved the feeling of having a tan and looking healthier. Ironic!

Five years isn't a long time for a mole to turn cancerous, when you think I hadn't even had moles before I started using the sunbeds. It shows how often I went, and how addicted I became to the pursuit of brown, glowing skin. I went three times a week, and sometimes even five times! Way too much!

I'd always hated looking pale. It's not that I've got anything against pale skin, but I felt that a tan suited me better. My sessions at the tanning salon were an integral part of my overall beauty regime, and I loved that sun-kissed, carefree, tanned look. Maybe it's because I love summer so much.

Each time I went I was on the machines for twelve minutes at a time, which is pretty full on.

Mum had spotted my misshapen mole while I lay in bed one morning at uni. She peered at my knee, saying, 'That one looks a bit funny; perhaps you should get it checked out.' I shrugged, thinking it was a fuss over nothing, but to assuage her I agreed to go to the GP. My GP looked at it and decided it was probably fine, but just in case, I would be referred to a dermatologist. I wasn't bothered. The mole hardly looked as if it had changed at all, really. It looked more like it had been smudged. It wasn't hideous or weeping, nothing like that. It just looked a weird shape.

The dermatologist said the same. Probably nothing to worry about. No one seemed very concerned about it at all. I started to think Mum might have been overreacting a bit, but I understood that she would always be a bit more alert to any issues or problems with me after what had happened. I was glad to put her mind at rest – or so I thought!

'Christ, Jordan, haven't you been through enough?' Mum was angry now. She stared into the garden, her lips twisted with unsaid words.

I wheeled over to her and put my hand on hers.

'I don't think we can take any more. I feel like this is your rock bottom, Jordan. All I can say is that you must have some pretty harsh karma to burn off!'

I smiled at that. Mum's sense of humour hadn't entirely fled her. 'It's going to be OK, I know it is. How many bad things can happen to one person, you know? Must be my turn to be OK, I reckon.' I wanted desperately to reassure her.

'I knew I was putting myself at risk going on the sunbeds, and this is the result. I won't use them again. From now on I'm only using fake tan.'

'Yes, but is it too late, Jordan?' Mum gave my forehead a swift kiss before turning back to the kitchen work surface where she switched on the kettle, her back to me, leaving me unable to think of anything to say. Instead I looked out of the window. It was the kind of sweet, benign summer day fond memories are made of, not the kind of day you get bad news.

The procedure to cut the cancer out was very straightforward. Mum took me to the hospital. We sat in the waiting room, Mum flicking through a magazine without reading the pages.

'Jordan Bone, come through.' The receptionist pointed us in the direction of the dermatologist's room. Mum wheeled me in.

'Are you OK with needles?' asked the kindly nurse, and I nodded.

After the local anaesthetic was given to me, the doctor performed the surgery, taking off a layer of skin cells from the area around the site of the original mole.

'We're sending this off to the lab for them to do a biopsy.

We'll know more in a few days.' My GP was very straight-forward. We said goodbye and went home.

To be honest, I hadn't expected to hear anything more about it. Then one day a few weeks later, the phone rang and it was my doctor. The biopsy results had come back. I admit that by then I was feeling anxious. I'd realised the gravity of the situation, that this could make or break my recovery.

To help myself I'd been meditating as preparation, to find some serenity within myself to counter whatever was coming. I wanted to feel that I would cope either way. My GP gave me the verdict over the phone. I could hear him smiling, and before he spoke a word I just knew everything was OK.

'It's good news. I won't keep you in suspense. The biopsy of the skin around your knee shows that we did indeed catch the cancer in time. You're a lucky girl, Jordan,' he said. He wasn't being ironic, and actually I did feel unbelievably happy to hear the news. This wasn't another fatal blow. I was cancer-free. It felt like a miracle.

'You'll have to come in for a check-up every six months from now on, but I'm happy to say it looks like the cancer was completely localised, and I don't have any worries about it.'

I was so young to be told such an awful thing; that at the age of twenty I had cancer. I know I am one of the lucky ones. I feel so thankful that I was spared another blow to my health, and want to really hit home to you guys that skin cancer kills people. In fact, more than two thousand people a year die, many of whom are sun-worshippers or tan-chasers, like I was. Sunbeds emit mostly UVA rays, not UVB, which are the ones that cause sunburn. However, both can cause DNA damage and lead to skin cancer, and the rays from a sunbed can be as powerful as midday sun.

Going on sunbeds gives you a 60 per cent greater chance of getting skin cancer than if you'd never used one. That's massive, and really scary.

Wearing fake tan is the only safe option now, as I still love the look and feel of bronzed skin. It reminds me of summer holidays as a child, happy days running through Grandad's garden, splashing in my paddling pool at home or out on my pink bike. I guess I've always equated sunshine with freedom.

Since I had that mole taken off my leg, I've had another six moles removed from other parts of my body. It brings it home how it's always best to be safe in the sun. Put your factor fifty on and look after yourself! And it's not just about the skin cancer if you use sunbeds. It ages you! It dries out your skin and gives you wrinkles. And I don't need *those* yet, thank you very much.

I was so lucky to catch it in time, but it can happen to anybody. Remember that you're important, and you're worth spending the time it takes putting on fake tan.

I broke my neck, and then got skin cancer. That's pretty

unlucky! Yet the experience taught me so many lessons. It was a real wake-up call to live my life and not waste a second of it. I realised that this life is my one chance of being 'me', if that makes sense, and I want to live the best life I possibly can. I deserve it. *You* deserve it too. Be the very best 'you' you can.

The cancer diagnosis was shocking, but I had found a new way to deal with what life throws at me by staying focused and positive. I understood that there is always a way round things, and despite things going wrong, there is nothing to hold you back – nothing. I learnt to switch my negative thoughts to positive ones through meditation. I focused on mindfulness, which meant I became conscious of the thoughts as they came. I realised that's all negative thoughts really were; they were just wonky thoughts, and they meant nothing, so why not change them to nice thoughts? It took a while.

I meditated every day for months, spending time shifting the shape of my inner feelings, and it really worked, so much so that I went back to my GP, but this time to ask to come off the antidepressants.

'I think it's time to stop my medication. It's been helpful, but I'm doing so much positive stuff these days, I feel so much happier and more able to get by,' I told my GP.

He'd replied, 'Are you sure, Jordan? You've come through a lot. I don't want you to stop the medication if it's working for you. You might be doing too much at once.'

I could see what he meant, but I was adamant. I was recognising my own strengths and I knew I was ready. It was more like an instinct, but I also knew I had the tools given to me by my online guided meditation sessions to help me if I needed it. So I cut down quite quickly, and within a couple of months I was free of the drugs.

I would always say to anyone with depression that it's best to seek proper medical help rather than suffer in silence. That's what I had to do, and it helped. Just because it was right for me to come off antidepressants, it doesn't mean I'm advocating stopping drugs that might be right for you. Always take your doctor's advice.

I also turned my cancer around by making a video called 'Why I Fake Tan' to try and get that message across to others, and to show how dangerous sunbeds can be. I'm worth more than putting my body at risk – and so are you.

Nowadays I use bronzer on my face as well as a bit of fake tan. I like to subtly warm up my skin without looking too orange!

My preferred product is bronzing powder, and I apply it using a fat brush that smooths over my foundation and concealer. Bronzer is used for warming up the skin (but if it's not too warm you can also use it to contour).

There's nothing nicer than a sun-kissed face, whether you like a touch of warmth or, like me, a strong summer glow. To me it represents health and vitality, and it helps me to feel that way just by applying product!

I could have looked back at my sunbed use with regrets. I could have been really hard on myself, blaming myself for getting cancer. But I don't do that any more. I forgave myself for doing what I did, and I learnt from the experience. From the day I got that phone call I've never used a tanning salon again. Instead I switched to fake tan, although I'm happy with or without it. There are so many awesome brands out there now. You won't look streaky or orange, I promise!

My cancer showed me – as if I didn't already know – that we only have one life to live, and that knowing that can be the spur to achieve great things. It's pointless regretting our actions. Things happen for a reason, and we have to learn from them and move on.

Don't waste your life in fear or regret – there's so much more to you. Pick yourself up. Dust yourself down, and go for it!

15

Hair

Letting it Down!

'Follow your heart, always.'

'That guy Mike is pretty hot,' giggled my friend. We were in a cheeky mood that evening and were eyeing up the local lads.

'Come on, don't scare him off!' I grinned. My friend turned and grimaced before knocking back the last of her vodka and Diet Coke. 'Well, I'm off for a dance. Come on, Jordan!'

'Yay, let's have fun!' I hollered back at her.

Two gorgeous girls, all glammed up to the nines with straightened, glossy hair, full make-up and lacy tops with tight jeans and heels, with me in the front leading the way to the dance floor. I *love* dancing, even in my chair, so I was always the first up. We were on a mission to have a good time.

We jostled through the moving crowd of people dancing. My wheelchair made it easier for us, as people always sprang out of the way as soon as they saw a disabled person coming! It was hot and loud in there among the heaving, braying dancers.

The music in the club was pounding. Before I left I gestured for another drink, a Disaronno and Diet Coke, and whooped as one of my favourite tracks started playing.

'Yeah! Let's go!'

It was a Thursday night, our regular night out in King's Lynn, and it was a welcome chance for me to let my hair down, figuratively speaking, and enjoy myself.

I looked over to where Mike was standing, surrounded by his mates. They were all dressed up, too, wearing designer-brand shorts and T-shirts or well-cut jeans and trousers. Mike had his back to me now, so I focused on the music, moving my chair and feeling the beat by moving my neck in time to the rhythm.

'He is gorgeous, but I've think he's a bit of a lad, one of the RAF boys. Definitely not my type!' I shouted over the music when we'd all stopped dancing and had come back to the edge of the dance floor where we'd based ourselves.

I was never one of those girls who is always looking for a boyfriend. And since my injury, I was wary of letting anyone in as I didn't want to waste time with someone who might mess me around. I wasn't worried about being single; I was living life on my terms as much as I could these days, having fun again, going out and recording my videos. What did I need a boyfriend for?

I know people might think I was scared that no one would approach me because I was in a wheelchair, but I honestly didn't give that a second thought. What you see is what you get with me, and in some ways, the chair made that easier. I couldn't exactly hide my disability; it was on public view, so I knew that if anyone did ever like me they'd have got past the wheelchair part of things already.

'No, definitely not my type at all,' I finished, throwing a sly glance back over to where the guys were standing nearby.

Later in the evening, we went into a random kebab shop. I wheeled myself in and looked over to the counter. The same group of lads from the club was there. Mike was there as well. Instantly he smiled at me. I smiled back at him nicely, just wanting to be friendly.

I hadn't had lots of boyfriends prior to the crash, and I was definitely not looking for one now. I also knew that I didn't want a short-term fling with a lad like Mike, however drop-dead gorgeous he was. I wanted to wait for the real thing, and yes, he was attractive, but I knew he hung out with guys who liked being out drinking and partying a lot. I loved my weekly nights out, but these lads were at it all the time, or so I'd heard. Not my style at all.

But he *was* good-looking, I'll admit that! Mike was tall, with a toned body (he always wore super-tight T-shirts, which I have teased him about ever since!) and dark hair.

'Right, I'm going over to him.' I giggled to my pal, who shushed me, and together we looked at Mike, who humoured me and turned away. Something about that gesture made me wonder if he was as laddish as he seemed.

'I'd better introduce myself,' I said, and right there and then I went and told him my name before we left the shop.

That was where it all started.

Over the next few months, I saw him loads of times in bars and clubs, but we'd never spoken. Then in March 2011, we were in Chicago's, a cheesy club in the town. I was just out with Kirsty. By then I'd decided that I actually quite liked Mike, as he'd never once tried to chat me up, but I knew he was interested because he couldn't stop staring at me!

I decided to take the bull by the horns and go over to him instead. I've always been like that. If I think something needs saying, I'll say it. I guess by then, after months of not quite getting to know him, I decided that night that it was overdue.

His face broke into a soft smile as I wheeled over. He had been pretending he hadn't seen me, but I kept catching him looking out of the corner of my eye.

'Hi,' I said. I smiled at him.

'Hi, erm, can I buy you a drink?' he replied, his voice rather gruff.

'Sure, Disaronno and Coke, please, and I think my friend

Kirsty wants one as well,' I said boldly. That made him laugh. I guess he wasn't expecting me to be so cheeky!

Mike got his debit card out of his wallet. He was really drunk, and instead of going to the bar himself he just offered it to Kirsty, who was standing nearby. She looked at me, shrugged, then grinned, coming back a few minutes later with a round of drinks.

'Should've bought champagne!' I shouted above the music.

That broke the ice.

'Would you pass me my drink, please?' I said to Mike. Kirsty had wandered off, leaving the drinks at the far edge of the table.

'No, get it yourself,' was his unexpected reply!

'Uh, well, I can't, because I'm paralysed!'

Mike looked at me. I honestly don't think he'd really taken in my situation, despite the chair and my curled-up hands.

'Oh, OK,' was all he replied, pushing my drink towards me. I wasn't offended. In fact I thought it was hilarious that he really hadn't cottoned on. Mike looks back and says he was so besotted by me that he really didn't notice, but whether that's true or not I don't know!

We sat and chatted for the rest of the evening. Mike seemed sweet. He was definitely one of the guys, but he also seemed quite shy as well. He was twenty-three, and was an aircraft engineer in the RAF. He was based at Marham, which wasn't far away, about half an hour's drive from King's Lynn.

At the end of the night, Mike asked for my number and we arranged to meet for a casual drink in the week.

The day of our first 'date' (though it wasn't an official one, it was more just two people getting to hang out together), I hadn't heard from him but I wasn't worried. He'd seemed too keen to blow me out. I made a big effort to look casual, but in reality I had my carer blow-dry my hair and curl it. I put a full look on my face, with dark, smoky eyes, nude lips and peach-toned blush.

When I was sure I was ready to leave, I sent him a text: *Hey Mike, I'm leaving now. Will you be there soon?*

There was a pause before he texted back. *Left my wallet at work. Gonna have to rearrange. Sorry Jordan*

I was incensed.

Perhaps he was just a player, mucking me around? He had no idea of the effort I'd gone to to get myself made up and ready to see him. My blood was boiling. I watched television for the rest of the evening feeling really grumpy and let down.

Then around 11 p.m., I relented and texted: *What you up to? X*

He replied: *I'm watching The O.C. You? X*

The O.C. was my favourite programme, *ever*. I grinned when I read his message, thinking, *oh, maybe I'll give him another chance – he might be all right after all!*

From that day onward he texted me every day.

How are you?

Fancy hooking up tonight?

What you doing?

Literally every day I got some kind of message from him.

The first time he came over, we hung out together in the lounge. He wouldn't even sit next to me. I had to tell him to come and sit by me on the sofa!

'So, do you want to do this again?' Mike asked as he made to leave. It was almost 1 a.m. I was shattered, but we'd spent all night just talking, and it was amazing how natural I felt with him and how we had so much in common. We loved the same shows and movies, and Mike was thinking of setting up as a fitness instructor in the future, so health and beauty were combined passions, as was positive thinking. It was quite strange just how much we connected on.

'Yeah, I'd really like that,' I answered, and waited. He suddenly looked lost for words. He stood up, and neither of us spoke.

I couldn't bear the tension, so I said, 'Can I have a hug?' God, that feels so cringey now!

He hugged me, then he stalled. The moment seemed to go on forever. The sparks between us were real, and I knew by now that he liked me. I felt like I would burst with anticipation, so I said, 'For God's sake, just kiss me!'

I can't believe I had the nerve! He laughed, then leant in and we had our first kiss. It was lovely. He was lovely. I spent the next few days mooning about until our next night out together, which was a meal at an Italian restaurant in the centre of town.

This was a big deal, as I would be going without a carer, with Mum on speed dial at home ready to come out to help me if I needed her.

'Would you take me there a bit earlier, Mum?' I asked, sipping my coffee. 'Yuck, this has gone cold.'

'Do you want me to heat it up for you? I can put it in the microwave. It'll just take ten seconds.

'Course I'll take you earlier. We can get you settled, sort your coat out, don't worry. I'll just be at the end of the phone if you need me.'

Mum looked at me tenderly. This was exciting for her as well. I was like a fledgling bird leaving the nest, though for the second time.

I beamed gratefully.

'Thanks, Mum. All I've got to do now is decide what to wear . . . Aargh, I've got nothing new.'

Mum had to laugh at that. I loved my clothes, and I had rails full of outfits.

In the end, after much deliberation, I plumped for a long-sleeved, floaty cream dress which was quite short, and a cute pair of heels. My carer used my straightening irons on my hair to curl it, first covering it in a cloud of heat protection spray.

*

My hair has always been my crowning glory. I'm really fussy about how I wear it, and it's been great to find carers who can make it look the way I would've done it. On days when my hair doesn't look great, I try to make up for it with my make-up.

To me, having good hair is an essential part of looking and feeling good. I always use a quality shampoo and conditioner, as the basis for it looking healthy, and have regular cuts. Before using the straighteners, curling or blow-drying, I always apply a product like the hair protector.

Then when the style is complete – either waves or straight – I use a texturising, volumising hairspray. I like maximum volume! There are other ways to get volume into your roots without the need to backcomb, which just kills your hair. A spritz of sea-salt spray does the job, as do root-booster powders, dry shampoo or even putting in large rollers to make it extra big, giving it volume from the root. I always go for the high-impact look, even if I'm toning down my make-up. I love my hair looking glam. Big hair is always a winner with me!

One trick to create the kind of bouncy, voluminous waves that I love is to use a curler. It's amazing. Mine has three different heads, and I use the largest, a 32 mm head, to create waves rather than curls. You can also choose which temperature to set it at. I use 180 degrees, then my carer separates my hair into three sections. Taking an inch or so of hair at a time, she curls the lock round the brush head, holding it against the heat for two to five seconds. That's usually plenty of time! Don't want to fry my hair! Each piece of hair should be wound round the head in opposite directions so that the curls don't form a clump together. It means the hair is fuller. Once it's cool (this hardly takes any time at all), it's brushed through to get the kind of soft waves I adore.

Most of the time I wear my hair down, but I do have days when a simple pony feels right. My hair is smoothed back and held with a band, then sprayed with a soft-hold hairspray to keep the strands in place.

When my carer had finished, I double-checked my reflection in the mirror. It was a Thursday night, the night I usually got dressed up, and that evening was no different. I had gone for a Barbie-pink lip, a defined wing with liquid eyeliner and fake tan – quite a dramatic look, as I wanted to make an impression.

'OK, Jordan, ready to go?' Mum poked her head round the door.

'Yep, here I am, all good,' I sang back at her. I was feeling excited about the meal. It was mine and Mike's first proper date, even though he says we were only 'official' on 16 April 2011, when he announced we were together to his friends and family.

Mum drove me to the restaurant and wheeled me in, settling me at my table. The staff, who knew me, brought over my drink with a straw so I could sip it myself. I had about ten minutes to relax before Mike arrived.

When he walked in, my heart turned over. He looked gorgeous. He was wearing one of his tight All Saints T-shirts, showing off his muscly physique.

'Hey, Mike.'

'Hey, Jordan, you look lovely. I hope you're hungry.' He grinned, sitting opposite me.

He called over to the waiter and ordered himself a Diet Coke. I'd already got a drink, so instead he put a menu in front of me and studied his.

'I take it you're starving!' I laughed.

'Ravenous,' he answered with a huge smile. 'What do you fancy?'

I ordered what I always had there, a goat's cheese *al forno* pasta dish, because it was easy for me to eat. All I had to do was stab the pasta. I didn't have to ask anyone to cut it up for me. Mike ordered an Italian burger, and we chatted happily. It felt so easy with him; there were no weird gaps in the conversation. I felt like I'd known him ages.

Mum arrived just as the bill came, and so I made quite a quick exit, though not deliberately! Mike wasn't put off; he turned up at mine later that evening.

We kept seeing each other over the next couple of weeks, and it got to the point where I wanted to know what was going on.

'So, I've had a great night, Mike.'

'Yeah, me too,' said Mike, flicking through the TV channels.

'Look, there's something I need to say,' I said, feeling a little nervous.

'What's that, Jordan? God, there's nothing on the TV these days. Can't find any O.C. reruns anywhere,' he replied.

'I need to speak, Mike. You're really nice, and we have a great time together, but I'm not sure where this is going. I've had a lot of crap in my life, and I know this is probably a bit pushy, and I'm sorry if it is, but I'd really like to know what's happening between us.'

'Oh, I see,' answered Mike, running his fingers through his hair. For a moment he looked awkward, then he shrugged and just came out with it.

'I really like you, Jordan, and I'd like to hang out lots more with you,' he said. I could see he was trying to play it cool.

'That's nice, and I want to hang out with you, too, but I just want to say that I don't want to be messed around. If you don't see anything progressing with us, then perhaps it's best to leave it.' I hoped I wouldn't frighten him off, but at the same time, I knew I had to make my feelings heard. I was protecting myself from any unnecessary hurt.

I wouldn't have been devastated if Mike had said there was nothing going on. I had great people around me, an established routine and friends. I was OK with my life, and I was like, 'take me or leave me'. I wasn't going to pretend for anyone, but at the same time I knew I liked Mike – my heart was in this, and I didn't want to be mucked about.

His answer was to kiss me softly on the lips.

That put my mind at rest, but I also knew that even at that point Mike didn't know the extent of the help I needed, especially with personal things. When we started going further afield, a carer would come with us, like the time in the summer when we went to Hunstanton. We spent a day at the beach, playing bingo, and Mike even won a teddy, which he gave to me.

Our first trip away with just us was Woburn Safari Park in August of that year. By this time Mike was staying over pretty much every night, and so once we were both up, we got into my car, a black Audi, and Mike drove the two and a half hours to the park after lifting me in and storing my chair in the boot.

I was eager to go, but quite nervous about Mike taking care of me for the first time. I needn't have worried. I felt really safe with him driving, and we had such a laugh together. I was wearing my 'everyday' make-up look, with winged eyeliner, loads of mascara and a nude lip – and lots of fake tan, of course! I used to wear a strong brow with lots of brow pencil, making them very dark and defined. These days I prefer a softer look; in fact I think my brows back then looked rank!

But one thing they do show me is that I've evolved, just as my hair and make-up style has evolved, and that's good because it shows I'm constantly flexible and changing.

My hair was blow-dried into soft waves, and I wore a baby-yellow top with a frill round the bottom, red jeggings and flats.

Mike wore a designer grey T-shirt and beige chinos, and friendship bracelets around his wrist. I felt good just being sat next to him, as there was usually my wheelchair between us. Looking back at a photo we took of ourselves in the car, me pouting as usual and him looking very sultry – we look good together!

My heart always lifts when I see that picture. We're so well suited. We're both passionate about our work, and we both care about our appearance. How lucky was I to meet someone so perfect! I could be my true self with Mike; or perhaps it's just that I had come to a point where I knew who I was and what I wanted to achieve, and that spilled over into the rest of my life. Of course, sometimes we encounter difficulties due to my situation, but we are strong enough to overcome them.

At the park, we saw the tigers and giraffes, but the best bit was when we drove through the monkey enclosure. The monkeys jumped on all the cars, including ours, and made us laugh out loud, they were so sweet and naughty! I love animals. If I could, I'd have an animal sanctuary!

'Look, it's like, so human!' I squealed as a monkey jumped on the car in front of us. 'They're so cute. It's got real fingers and toes.'

Mike was practically hanging over the steering wheel to get a better view.

'He wants in, doesn't he? He's sat on the ledge!' he said.

'He wants a Pringle,' I laughed (we had some with us).

'I'm pretty sure he shouldn't eat crisps. Look at his face!' Mike added, and we both giggled.

It was a real treat. It felt like we were any other normal couple, and we returned home tired but happy. Mike moved in officially less than a month later, giving up his place in Marham. I hardly noticed the difference. Mike was there with me pretty much all the time!

I never expected to find someone like Mike at that point in my life; I was happy, as I've said, and so I was relaxed about whether I ended up with anyone or not.

It just shows that there are always obstacles in life – but it doesn't mean they can't be overcome. I've been able to let my hair down and live a great life – all because I didn't let my paralysis stand in my way. So much of my success has been down to following my heart, trusting in my own wisdom and intuition. We all have to do what makes us happy. It's as simple as that. Being with Mike, dressing up and looking ultra-glamorous makes me happy, so that's what I do.

Life is too short to be unhappy – trust me, I know!

16

Lips

Speaking Out

'Never be scared to speak out – you might even
make a difference if you do.'

I'm trying to speak but the words won't come out. 'Slow down, slow down!' I want to beg, but my lips won't work, my mouth gapes open but only air comes out. The car speeds up, time becomes elastic, stretches into this abyss. I know this is the end for me. Inside I'm screaming. Yet no noise comes out. As if in slow motion, the car skids. I clutch at nothing. My life rolls out before me as the car spins; every moment of joy, every memory, every kiss from Mum or chuckle from toddler Eden distorts and collapses in front of my vision. I don't want to die. This is what I want to say.

This is my message, but no sound comes out. My lips are silent . . .

I gasped, taking in short, choking breaths. I was dreaming about the crash, the moment where everything was lost. It had been almost eight years since the accident, but my overwhelming sense of powerlessness remained, though I never usually had nightmares or disturbed dreams. My lack of a voice, my fear at speaking out, my inability to demand that the driver stop the car, were all expressed through the repetition of those terrible few seconds before the car rolled over into the ditch. My lungs felt constricted. I panted to get oxygen into my body.

I was responding as if I really was back inside that vehicle again as it careered out of control.

A flashback, that's all it is, calm down, Jordan, it's not real, I repeated to myself, yet it was so vivid I could almost smell the fear, hear the sound of the stereo, see the trees rear up before me.

I tried to focus on the present day. I gave myself time for my breathing to return slowly to normal, for my pulse to stop racing, for my heart to slow. I watched as daylight seeped through the curtains of the room I now shared with Mike. We had a special bed, two flexible hospital-style single beds built together to make one huge double. Each bed could be raised and lowered via a push-button on each side. Mike was sleeping soundly next to me. I allowed myself to doze for a while, and it was during my half-sleep that I made the decision to speak out about my injury – and road safety.

A charity called Fixers, which gives young people a voice

and has the slogan 'young people using their past to fix the future', had contacted me in October 2012, asking me to share my experiences. They had got hold of me via Spinal Research (a charity that leads the way in finding a cure for paralysis caused by spinal cord injury). I had raised money for Spinal Research earlier in the year when an old college friend of mine, Sam, had contacted me. She worked for Barclays Bank, and they were doing a charity event. Whatever I raised on the night, the bank would match. At the time I was running a clothing company called Vintage Bones, which has since flopped, but before it did we put on a vintage fashion show with friends modelling on a catwalk, and which raised £1,300 for Spinal Research.

Sam was in the same media class with me at King's Lynn College, and she had been a good friend to me. Last year for my birthday she'd brought round afternoon tea for me. She is thoughtful like that.

Anyway, not long afterwards, Fixers found me. They wanted me to shoot a video for their website, which uploads films made by loads of young people talking about their differing experiences of life, whether it's being gay or trans-sexual, having an illness or family issues. I sat at my laptop, looking through the videos, stung to tears by the honesty and bravery of all the youngsters who were speaking about their troubles, but also about their hopes as well. It unlocked something within me.

I need to speak out about this, I thought to myself; *at*

least that way, if I help one driver not to take risks, or one person not to get into a car driven by a newly qualified driver, then my injury has been worth something.

Suddenly I saw a way to give back. I'd been helped by so many people in getting over my injury. Perhaps by talking about what happened I could change someone else's life for the better.

My first talk was scheduled at my old high school, Springwood, which was now an academy. I contacted them myself. It was a way for me to practise the series of talks that Fixers wanted me to do in schools. Also, my home-town school was closest to my heart, and I felt it was there that I wanted my message to start.

Pushing myself down the school corridor, I felt a pang of something like regret. I was sad that I hadn't been able to make going back there work for me. I was glad I'd left – I didn't regret that decision for a second – but it was a bittersweet moment, wheeling into the library to see pupils from different classes staring back at me, dressed in their new uniforms yet looking so much like me and my friends did all those years ago.

Instantly my mouth dried up. I felt terrified! Would the words come out? What would I say? I'd practised at home in my room, but it wasn't the same as sitting in my wheelchair in front of a sea of faces looking at me expectantly.

I cleared my throat, taking a sip from a proffered

glass of water with my usual straw balanced inside.

'Hey, guys, I'm Jordan Bone, and you might already have heard about me,' I started, desperately hoping the words would continue to flow!

'I'm here to tell you what happened to me, and how you can all keep safe on the roads . . .' I began.

The session was tiring. I talked for almost an hour, answering questions and telling them my story. I could see shock on some faces, pity on others. I knew that the sight of my chair might affect some of the younger ones quite deeply, so I made sure to be as upbeat as possible and give a positive finish to my tale.

'So, guys, that's what happens when you ignore your instincts and get into a car with someone who has only just passed their test. I'm sure a few of you have done it, and thank goodness you're OK, but you never know what might happen on the next trip, or the next.

'Look, I have a really fulfilling life. I've got loads of friends, a brilliant boyfriend and my amazing family. It's not all bad, by any stretch of the imagination, but things could have been a lot easier.'

One of the children shot up their hand.

'Yes, go on, ask me anything,' I said, smiling.

'Well, if you could be made to be not paralysed any longer, would you do it?' the student asked, her face flushing bright red as everyone turned to look at her.

I laughed, but answered very definitely: 'Of course I

would! Who wouldn't want their body back?

'Life isn't easy for me, but I am still myself despite the chair and my paralysis. But if you're asking me if there was a medical miracle and I could be cured tomorrow, then absolutely, yes I would.

'I'm not here to frighten you, but I do want you to realise that there are sometimes consequences we can't escape from. My disability is one of them.

'I should never have got in that car, but I didn't know the driver would try and race someone; I had no idea.

'I would give anything to be like you, with working arms and legs, but that's never going to happen. What I'm trying to say is that I've created a life out of all that. I've moved forward, even though I have this injury. Sometimes I have bad days, but that doesn't mean I have a bad life.

'I try to live as positively as I can so that better things happen to me. I still have choices, even though I'm paralysed. You have the choice to be safe, to not get into cars when you know you shouldn't. Just make sure you have the courage to make good choices for yourself. You owe it to yourselves.'

When I'd finished there was a brief moment of silence, and then the class started clapping. I sat there, my eyes blinded by tears, realising that whatever I'd just said, it was a good way of dealing with things. I may even have given some motivational tools to some of the children, and possibly stopped at least one young life from being affected by a road accident.

That was only the first session.

Several other classes were brought in for me to repeat my talk to. By the time I finished I could barely say a word, I was so shattered!

My carer took me home afterwards. I was buzzing from the experience, even though I was exhausted. That night I felt more tired than I had in ages. It took a lot out of me, but in a good way, a great way!

'You can do stuff with your life even if you struggle.' I think that was my overall message, I told Mike later that evening. He was filling up a glass of water for me.

'Sounds like you were brilliant. Will you do any more talks?' he asked, sliding my drink to me across the table and sitting down on the seat opposite me.

'D'you know what? I think I will!' I laughed. He leant over and kissed me on the lips. It had been a good day.

The next speaking gig with Fixers was at a construction college summer camp, which I did a couple of times. A girl from the charity met me there. The support and the help they gave me to speak publicly was the push that propelled me into what I do today.

In some ways I owe a lot of my success to the guys from Fixers. The charity has a special place in my heart, and always will. They helped me gain more confidence both in myself and in my message. That was the point at which the meditation and positive thinking videos became more meaningful to me.

I started to take what I did in my online vlogs seriously. Whereas before it was more about being part of a nice community, it now became something I could do with a view to having a career or a part to play in a wider world.

I gave what I could to those sessions, hoping I was making a difference. The most difficult, and worthy, talk I gave at the time was at a driving school in Chelmsford. That was hugely daunting. I was wheeled into a room full of at least a hundred young drivers and their parents. All eyes were on me. It was terrifying!

I was so glad I'd done the other talks so that I didn't freeze, though my voice was nervous and I could hear myself gasp a bit as I spoke. It was amazing, though, because that was where I got the most response. It was incredibly rewarding. As I talked, I felt that the young people were taking notice and listening to me. Some even had tears in their eyes!

I'll never forget one girl and her mum, sitting on the front row, who were both in tears by the time I finished. The girl didn't look old enough to be driving, but she smiled at me, making eye contact, as they stood up to leave. We didn't speak, but that definitely made an impact on me. I felt I'd reached out to someone and been heard. An incredible, life-defining moment.

I realised that public speaking, either via sessions like

those or vlogs on my YouTube channel, was what I was meant to do. That's when I felt most connected to people, and to my own journey.

Yet there was a part of me I hadn't yet incorporated into my videos, and it was in February 2013 that I created my first-ever make-up vlog.

Why hadn't I thought of doing it before? Make-up was my passion. I spent a fortune buying different brands and products, trying them out and perfecting my own techniques for applying them. Make-up is what helped me rediscover myself in hospital. That moment when I asked the nurses to help me pick up my mascara wand was actually the most pivotal point of my recovery, which may sound weird.

My accident had the most impact, obviously, but in terms of everything that's happened since, it was definitely my fight to apply make-up that defined my life – and my success! It was staring me in the face; I was so into looking good and wearing great brands and products. Why wouldn't my followers be interested in that as well as in my motivational speaking? I didn't have to think twice. I was quite excited about it.

Again, I was following my heart. So important, guys! It always leads in the right direction.

That day, my carer had come in and got me up at 8.30 a.m. Mike usually left the house at 6.30 a.m. to get to Marham, so I never saw him in the mornings back then. My carer did my leg stretches to stop my feet and toes stiffening up, then helped me to the shower.

Once I was clean and fresh, she brought me back to bed to lie down as I was dried. It's really important to be dried properly, otherwise pressure sores develop. Then I was helped into my usual clothes: a pair of black leggings and the grey jumper I'd picked out to wear on top. Once I was lowered into my chair, I was sat up as far back as possible so that I was balanced and my hips were straight, to avoid putting any stress on them. If I'm not straight in my chair I won't have as much stability, my neck will hurt and it will put more pressure on my side.

As my carer made breakfast, I'd check my emails and usually I'd think about what I wanted to say in my vlog, but that day I knew exactly what I'd do.

I'd decided I would show my followers my beauty haul – the products I used every day and that were, at the time, my favourites. I was having so much fun playing with make-up, and I wanted to share that with you guys out there! Little did I know that this new direction would pave the way for the amazing life I live now.

It seemed so natural to talk about the products. I mentioned the make-up I used then, in particular my gold YSL Touche Éclat Radiant Touch pen, which I couldn't live without! It's always in my handbag, even now. I told my viewers that my hands were paralysed, but that I could still use brushes to apply make-up. Perhaps because not that many people were watching me at the time, from this point onward after my make-up tutorials I got loads of messages asking why my hands didn't work, which led me to make my breakthrough video 'My Beautiful Struggle'. But that came later.

I showed my eyeliner pencil, from Mac, which was another product I felt I couldn't live without, as well as various Bobbi Brown, NARS and Makeup Academy products I was using that day to create my 'everyday' look.

Like I said, this was a different video for me. I love make-up, and that's one thing I could do independently. I couldn't do my own hair, as you know, which was (and still is) a bummer, but that day my carer had done it and it looked gorgeous, if I say so myself!

The response was great. People were watching my video and sending me messages saying they wanted to see more looks and have more tips. It really encouraged me to keep going. I also loved watching make-up tutorials on YouTube, so it was the obvious next step for me. I still rounded off my video by wishing my followers 'Peace, love and happiness'. I have always liked finishing on a high note.

From then on, the slant of my tutorials became about make-up, with some motivational videos thrown in when I felt I had something important to say.

Naturally I broke the news of my involvement in Fixers via a video on my channel on 30 April 2013, saying, 'When bad things do happen, you have to look at the positives and try to be the best person you can be, no matter what the situation is.

'I want to save lives. I want you to have the best life; I want you to realise how important you are and how important life is.' That sums it up for me!

Things started moving quickly.

In May 2013, at the age of twenty-three, I shot my video 'Amazing Not Invincible' with Fixers.

Sadly, I wasn't surprised when I learnt that road accidents are the single biggest killer of young people, the majority aged between seventeen and twenty-five, and mostly male drivers. I wanted young people to know the risks, as we only have one life and we have to make the most of it. I wanted to tell them that with a bit of common sense, their lives might be saved. I'm so proud of that video, and so honoured to have made a Fixers project.

If I save one life by doing it, then I know I will have done what I set out to achieve.

Just before I made the Fixers video, I had been given the chance to 'walk' again, for the first time in eight years, using a high-tech exoskeleton, at the Prime Physio specialist centre in Cambridge. I was strapped into an Ekso exoskeleton, in which, supported by a walking frame, and with my physio holding it behind me, I was able to take 645 steps! How amazing is that!

It was so weird to be upright. I felt really high up! Obviously I couldn't wear that every day, but it was good to be in that incredible piece of equipment. Mum and Mike both cried, they felt so emotional, and for the first time ever I was able to give Mike a hug standing up.

Our local paper, the *Lynn News*, called me a bionic woman after that!

My next big milestone was on 5 July 2013, when I published a vlog called 'The Authentic Me: Be Yourself!' It was a major step forward in my online career, and in my personal journey, showing that I was finally discovering who I was and having the courage to be myself, no matter what.

The past three years of YouTubing have formed a really important part of the journey for me in becoming more of the person I'm supposed to be, because I love make-up and I really enjoy doing beauty reviews and make-up-related videos. That's me! I've found it therapeutic.

My make-up changed from being experimental and quite dramatic to being more natural, then, when I gained more confidence, I worked lots of super-glamorous looks. When it came to my lips, I would pretty much always go for pink: a darker pink at night and a softer, nude-look pink for daytime.

Nowadays I use a liquid lipstick, which works really well for me. I do wear lip liners for a daytime look, depending on my lipstick. Nude lipsticks are my favourite.

Sometimes I think I'm buying the same colour, just from a different brand, but then I realise that although *nude* is a simple colour, there are so many different types of *nude* shades.

But there's something that's always been quite controversial on my channel – my use of lip fillers. I've had my lips injected with fillers since 2010, so for me it's not a big deal. It's something I wanted to try. I did it not because I was insecure, but because I wanted to.

It never lasts very long with me, probably because I was only using a little bit of product and I was metabolising it really fast. The first time I had it done I loved it; I thought it looked amazing, though I had to have anaesthetic injected into the inside of my mouth first! It was quite painful. Then I switched to numbing balm.

I've always wanted plump, juicy, full lips, so to me, it was a no-brainer to use fillers. When I've got bigger lips I think it complements my other features so much more than when they're thinner. I'm fine whether my lips are full or thin – it's just personal preference.

I once used a stronger version of the filler, a specialist product generally used for filling out cheeks and larger areas. I wanted it to last longer, so I took the plunge, having a double dose of the stiffer product. The therapist injected it into my top lip, then massaged it to break down any lumps. Once the swelling went down a few days later, she put a little bit more filler in to make my lips symmetrical, using a product that made things look softer. I loved the look! I haven't used the cheek filler since, but I would never tell someone not to do it if they wanted to.

It's a personal choice for me, and I know it's one that

doesn't resonate with everyone who subscribes to my channel. I'm not here to recommend it. It's just that I like being completely honest with my followers. They deserve to know the truth, and to me, it's nothing to be ashamed of. I *really* like having my lips fuller, and it's my body! There is some pain. My lips always ache immediately afterwards, but then the pain subsides. To me, it's worth it but to others it's not.

We should *all* be ourselves, and we should never try to be any different from who we are. Just be yourself. I felt so much more authentic once I had started putting my love for make-up into my vlogs. I realised at last that I was happy with who I was. And particularly in terms of the Fixers video and talks I did, I felt like people were finally listening to me. I was speaking out, and being heard.

Because I was a young person, others related to me, seeing me really hit the message home that you are 'amazing, not invincible'. I designed wristbands made with that message, to raise awareness of spinal injury. I realised that by sharing my story through the charity, I could inspire other young people. That was the beginning of everything.

I also appeared on ITV News, as I was involved in another Fixers project, the Fixers Carnage Road Safety Fixumentary, in September of 2013. I sat on a panel with other people whose lives had been affected by road accidents. We were debating how to change things to prevent others suffering the same fate.

One girl had lost her sister; another lost her boyfriend

in a motorbike accident. Hearing their stories brought everything back: those first days in hospital, the catastrophic news, the desperate hope and deep despair. I wasn't alone in feeling those things, sadly.

The heat that day was intense, and I was worried I would overheat as I can't sweat when I'm hot. I felt quite out of my depth. I didn't have statistics to hand about road deaths or accidents, but I wasn't there to give those. I was there to share from my heart. Many famous faces were in the audience listening to all of us speak, including TV presenter Gary Lineker and the actor Tyger Drew-Honey.

On another occasion I was invited to Transport for London, to sit on a focus group to talk about improving road safety. That one was even more stressful! I felt like there were loads of important people there, and the pressure got to me. So much so I started having a panic attack. I got through it with some deep breathing, and the conviction that I had an important message to share. Yes, and positive thinking! I *can* do this, I *can* do this, I repeated over and over as I waited to go into the room where I was speaking.

Saying our truth is often scary, but who are we if we don't? I had to gather together my courage again to speak out, but I had no option. I couldn't turn down the chance to influence even one person. If one young person was saved from a fate like mine, then it was all worth doing.

17

Brows

Raising Eyebrows

Don't be afraid to make an impact!

'Oh my God, I've been asked to appear on Pixiwoo's #Tues-dayChats!' I was beside myself. So happy.

Mike looked at me blankly.

'It's a huge deal. Everyone loves Pixiwoo. They've been on YouTube like, forever, and now they want to speak to me.'

Mike's face lit up. He hadn't got a clue what I was talking about, but clearly he was just really pleased for me.

Pixiwoo was one of my favourite YouTube channels, a make-up site for all ages run by sisters Sam and Nic Chapman. I'd been following them for ages, and couldn't believe they wanted me on their Tuesday Chats series! They literally had hundreds of thousands of followers on Twitter, Instagram and YouTube, and it meant exposure for me in a totally different league.

The morning of my chat came and I took extra-special care with my make-up, making sure I had hot, pouty, pink lips, slicked with gloss, and super-glam straight hair. I needed to look good!

My segment was called 'Staying Positive with Jordan Bone', and as soon as we went live I instantly felt relaxed. It was just like hanging out with the girls! I spoke about my injury, but we moved on to talking about my channel, my blogs, make-up tutorials and motivational speaking.

'How do you stay positive?' was the question that really struck me. I answered, talking about my family and my meditation that got me out of depression, but I also acknowledged that my character is at the heart of what spurs me on. I am an optimist – it's who I am. It was great to recognise that!

I also mentioned how Katie Piper, the amazing woman who turned her life around after a vicious sulphuric acid attack left her face badly burnt, had written an article about me in NOW magazine the previous November. Katie had named me as her Real Life Hero. Wow!

'It was a surprise, as I didn't know she was going to write it. Someone tweeted me, so I went out and got one [a copy], then she tweeted me!'

I wrote about it in my blog on my site jordansbeautifullife.

com: 'At first I thought it was a mistake and the person emailing me meant *LOOK* magazine, as I was featured in there the previous month.

'Anyway, I picked up a copy and turned to the inspirational and beautiful Katie Piper's column, and there I was. I am so honoured to be acknowledged by Katie because she is a massive inspiration, and all round a fab woman! Thanks for this, Katie, it made my week!'

Being on Pixiwoo was a chance to spread my message far and wide, though I had to mention my limitations: 'There is a lot more planning involved with my life. My boyfriend and I can't just go away for a night; I have to make sure someone is with us. It's not ideal. I could easily be down about it. You can't dwell on things; you have to keep upbeat.

'Doing all this on YouTube, doing my blog, trying to get myself out there, I just want to make a difference. I want to be successful as well. I want to make my mark on the world. What's the point in just plodding along? I want to make a difference to somebody, at least one person.'

Chatting about my school talks, I added: 'I don't want anyone else to go through what I went through, because I went through hell.

'I want them to be aware. A lot of them seem to be really taken aback by it and they seem to really listen as well.

'Hopefully it makes an impact on people, somehow.'

'What path did you see your life going down, and what

path has it changed to?' came the question. I stalled for a moment, before answering that one.

'It's hard to tell. I was only fifteen years old, and I don't think you ever know exactly what you want to do. I feel I'm still me. I'm one of those people who would probably be quite stubborn – I'd want to do what I want to do.'

At the end of the interview, the sisters Sam and Nic told their viewers to check out my YouTube channel, saying, 'It's amazing, and totally inspiring.'

Massive praise!

And wow, you did all check it out. Overnight my subscribers doubled to 10,000! In one day!! I was so touched, and so excited about this that I made a special vlog saying thank you to everyone who'd joined me on YouTube. I really felt I was getting out there and starting to make an impact. I was raising eyebrows – in a good way!

My brow products are probably the most essential in my make-up bag. The few times I've ever gone out without my brows on (!) I've felt really strange, not me at all!

Enhancing my eyebrows was one of the most difficult skills to reacquire, as they need to be even and they must look fairly identical, for obvious reasons. I have always liked to darken my brows quite dramatically, filling in my sparse brows and making them look much fuller and more defined than they actually are. I liked using a 'spooly' to brush the hairs in the right direction, and building on the colour and shape of them with brow pencil, my favourite at the time being one by Mac.

Nowadays I use a brow pomade in taupe with a small, angled brush, a relatively new product that is specially created to paint brows without making them look too obviously coloured. Pomade is a cross between a cream and a gel, and it is super-creamy and quite tricky to apply.

I have progressed so much that I can now place the brush into the hollow created between the frozen fingers of my hand myself. I use my mouth to reposition and twist the applicator so that I have it at an angle that suits me. I lean my head forward. Slowly and carefully I follow the shape of the brow, creating that nice full look I like.

When I used to wear brow pencil, I would start at the tail of my brow, nudging the creamy point of the pencil along and up to the front where my brow becomes larger and more prominent. I made sure the colour was graduated at the front so that the brow was not too big, but just the right shape. It was important for me to get this part of my look right. It set the tone for the whole of my face. Wonky eyebrows are never a good look!

It was always a badge of honour to me to be able to do something quite intricate by myself. (Although we must remind ourselves that brows are 'sisters', not 'twins', so will never be identical. As long as they don't look like 'distant cousins', we are all good!)

With the brow pomade nowadays, I hold the brush

between both clenched hands and move it sideways. I then move my head to create marks at the start of the brow, above the inner corner of my eye. This demarcates the end of the brow. It defines where things start and finish. Today I'm a bit lighter with my brows, a bit subtler, though I still like them to have a clear shape and texture.

It's good to change and evolve our styles. You can constantly refresh who you are and what you look like. We don't have to be set on one look, or one way of doing things. Be flexible. Experiment. It's all about having confidence in yourself and your looks, and, of course, it's fun too! And don't forget – the only drama you need in your life is make-up!

Strong brows make me feel empowered and positive, and these are the feelings that I want to filter through into all aspects of my life.

By the time of my twenty-fifth birthday in October 2014, things were definitely on the up.

I'd been wondering what Mike would get for me, hoping perhaps for some new make-up or a voucher so that I could buy some. What he gave me was a million times better . . .

'We're going to Paris? You're not kidding, right? We're actually going to Paris together?' Honestly, I think my voice rose a few octaves with excitement!

Mike nodded. 'Yep,' was all he said.

'Oh my God, that's so romantic! What's going on? You're

not normally so lovey-dovey! I'm joking, right?' I laughed.
I'd always wanted to go to the French capital – and what
could be nicer than going with the boyfriend I totally loved?
I'd been to EuroDisney, near Paris, as a nine-year-old, but
this was altogether different.

Mike had given me a guide to the city for my birthday
with a padlock in its packaging. I'd looked at him, puzzled.

He smiled. 'I'm whisking you off to Paris. We're going
there together, it's all sorted, and I'm taking you to the "love
lock" bridge.'

Love Lock Bridge, or the Pont de L'Archevêché as it was
really known, was where couples placed a padlock and
threw the key into the River Seine, symbolising their being
locked together forever. I'd mentioned to Mike that I
wanted to go there one day.

'That's so cool, I don't know what to say.' I was bowled
over. I couldn't believe my boyfriend had gone to so much
trouble to do something so special.

'OK, so just kiss me instead . . .' Mike replied.

We had already been abroad. In April of that year, we flew
to Miami for two weeks with Mum and Eden, for me to
attend the Brucker Biofeedback Centre to help me with my
muscles. Basically, biomechanical measurements are taken
using an EMG machine, which is seen in real time when I'm
using the muscles. This means information can be gathered
to help repair or rework muscles after injury.

For my first session, the therapist put sticky pads on my shoulders with wires coming off which attached to a computer. As I held the muscles I watched the green lines shoot up and down according to the intensity of the hold. The doctor, a nice American lady, said, 'With spinal injury you're going to tire more easily.'

And she was right!

I spent the first afternoon chilling by the pool in my bikini, after eating pancakes, as I was totally worn out. My second session of biofeedback was less stressful, so we went shopping afterwards, ending up in The Cheesecake Factory. Mike carried me into the sea on our third day, and we all ended up a bit red from sunbathing! I swooped up all the Jordana Best Lash Extreme Volumizing mascaras from the drugstore make-up section – it was recommended by another beauty guru and it was cheap.

Each day was progressively harder work, though, squeezing and holding my shoulder muscles, biceps and triceps. Despite this, we still caught a Miami Heat basketball game. It was awesome! Something we'd never done before. The next day was spent watching street performers, with the largest cocktails you've ever seen. By this stage, my body got achy and my wrists were sore.

The biofeedback took its toll. I hurt my hand. It was overstretched and it swelled up badly. I needed an X-ray. It was really annoying, as one of my fingers was stretched out too much, so I couldn't push my chair properly. Aside from that, I was so sad to leave Miami. We loved hanging out on Ocean Drive, soaking up the sun at the beach or the pool, going shopping when it was stormy.

'Push, push, push, that's it. I guess you do better when you're filmed!' the therapist laughed, encouraging me to squeeze my back muscles as far as I could. Mike was filming my vlog, showing my followers each part of my journey. Ever since we'd got together officially, Mike had been supporting me through everything.

The visit to Miami passed by in a whirlwind of activity – so many amazing experiences were packed in, and I was so glad to have Mike by my side.

The next few days before Paris were a thrill of making plans, looking online to see where we'd visit and deciding what to pack. A week later, just before we were due to leave, Mum was helping me get ready.

'Katie thought Mike might propose when we're out there.'

'Do you think so?' Mum replied.

'I don't know; it's pretty romantic. And I'd said to Mike ages ago that I wanted to go to the bridge. He's waited a while to do this, so maybe . . .' I said, trying not to flash a huge smile at Mum. 'Probably shouldn't expect it, though. If he doesn't, I'll probably be really disappointed!'

Mum was holding my make-up bags, trying to tuck them in between some cute flats and a creamy wool top.

'No, best not to get carried away. It would be wonderful, though, wouldn't it!' Mum's eyes twinkled.

'Don't encourage me, I'm already thinking about what kind of ring I would like, ha, ha, ha!' We both burst into fits of giggles, just as Mike poked his head round the bedroom door.

'Ready to go? Hey, what's so funny? Share the joke,' he said, sitting on the end of our bed.

'Nothing!' Mum and I replied in unison. We glanced at each other and started laughing again.

Mike sighed. 'OK, OK, come on, let's go. We've got Paris to conquer!'

'Ready in ten!' I called to him as he slouched out.

Hopping on Eurostar was so easy. I was wheeled through with no problems, and we settled into our Standard Premier seats. Lunch was served, which was a baguette (of course!), two types of cheese and oatcakes and grapes. Really yummy. We washed it all down with a couple of glasses of rosé wine, which made the two-hour journey pass very pleasantly.

We arrived in the 'city of love' at the Gare du Nord, which was incredibly beautiful, with iron gables soaring over our heads. Mike steered me through the swell of people, and I was dumbstruck by how large and ornate it was. We hopped in a cab and got to our hotel, the Fontaines du Luxembourg in the 6th Arrondissement.

The hotel was quaint and quite quirky, with fountains and rock-effect walls, some painted in strong colours, and huge murals of columns and fantastical countryside scenes – it was bizarre, but we loved it, especially the walk-in shower, which suited me perfectly.

'This place is amazing,' I shouted through to Mike as he showered, 'really weird, but I love it!'

'Glad you like it – I thought it suited us down to the ground,' he replied, poking his soapy head round the door.

'Get a move on, we haven't got all day. I'm starving,' I giggled back at him. He pulled a face and disappeared again, while I sat and took it all in.

Who could ever have imagined that I would end up in the most romantic city in the world with my gorgeous boyfriend? Life really is amazing. Things can turn around completely – you just have to have faith and know that they always get better.

I touched up my face, redrawing my brows and dusting my complexion with a tiny amount of loose powder, then spritzing some setting spray on so that my look would stay in place.

I dressed in a black leather jacket, a colourful dress, black tights and black ankle boots. I had made sure I'd fake-tanned the night before, so was looking just like I'd flown in from a holiday in the Caribbean!

To finish the look, I created a deep-pink lip, which complemented my hot-pink tote bag. Mike pulled on a trendy T-shirt, his leather jacket and a pair of black jeans, and we were ready to go out.

After we'd eaten, we stumbled on a really bizarre place called L'Urgence, which was a hospital-themed bar. Mike went up to the bar and ordered our drinks. We sat down and waited for them to arrive. Moments later, the bargirl placed them on our table – they were in baby bottles!

'Is this a fetish bar?' I whispered to Mike.

His face was a picture. Neither of us knew what to make of it all!

'God, I hope not! If it is, we're getting out of here,' Mike replied. He glanced round at the other drinkers. Most people looked fairly normal, quite a few touristy-looking people dressed in Halloween gear, perhaps, but no one was dressed up as a baby or anything as hilarious as that! There were a few witches, a warlock and someone who definitely looked mummified, but no nurses or bedpans in sight!

'I think we're safe. If they come and ask us to change into our nappies, we'll know to get the hell out,' joked Mike.

'It is a bit weird. Look, the cocktails are called things like "Tampax", "Colonic", "Laxative" and "Viagra"! Most random cocktail names ever,' I snorted into my drink, almost swallowing it down the wrong way.

'Gah, well, at least the beer's good. We should've brought our Halloween outfits, though, I can't believe we forgot the date!' I said, thinking it might have been good to get dressed up.

We'd arrived on the thirty-first, Halloween night, and the city was definitely in a party mood. After a few drinks we headed back to the hotel, wanting an early start for our first full day in Paris.

The next day dawned bright and clear. The sun was shining and the city was really warm, which made my choice of black jumper and tights perhaps not the best! After a leisurely breakfast of pastries, croissants and jam with hot tea, we left the hotel and decided to search for Love Lock Bridge on foot, me on my wheels!

The bridge's three stone arches spanned the Seine, linking the 4th Arrondissement and the Île de la Cité. It was an amazing sight. The road bridge was literally covered in thousands and thousands of locks, where people had placed them since the original love lock bridge, the Pont des Arts, was cleared of locks in 2010 because the weight of them threatened the bridge's structure. We ambled along, looking at the messages on the locks, many of them rusted by the weather but some gleaming as if they'd just been placed there.

'You know what, if I ever despair of human nature, I'll think of this bridge. There is so much love here, it's incredible.' I sighed. I was blown away by the spectacle. It was amazing how many locks were attached to the bridge. In fact, part of it was boarded up as it had started to collapse! It was so cute seeing so many declarations of love.

One of the messages read *Joe & Lucy, 22.10.14*; another, *Tash hearts Paul 2012*. They were all different sizes and colours, a cacophony of tributes to the human heart. Mike wrote our names and drew a heart on our padlock. So sweet.

'You choose where to put ours,' said Mike.

'Where should I put it?' I said, looking at the sea of locks.

'Wherever.'

He pushed me along a little further, and at that moment the sun seemed to increase in intensity, sparkling off the river and making the sky soar, an almighty blue above our heads.

'Here. Here is the perfect spot. Oh, and look, there's a pink lock. We have to put ours next to that one!' I smiled. 'Where is it, d'you have it?'

Mike grinned, fumbled around for it and produced it.

'OK, here goes, let's do this,' he said as he connected it to the rest of the bunch so that it sat next to the pink lock, nestled into the mass of padlocks. Then he turned the keys to lock it in place and threw them into the river. They sailed through the clear air and landed, plop, out of sight.

He leant over my shoulder and we kissed on the bridge. It was possibly the most perfect moment in my life.

There was a slight pause after the kiss, and that's when that little thought about him proposing gnawed its way back into my brain. I didn't want to say anything, though. I didn't want to spoil the moment. Mike had been incredible, surprising me with this trip. He'd planned everything, from the hotel and Eurostar to the bridge and our lock. I would never have said a word, but I know that deep down I felt a pull of disappointment. If there was ever a more perfect moment to ask me to marry him, then this was it. But we were happy, intensely happy. Our lives were ahead of us.

I looked round at the trees lining the river, framed in the background by the Notre-Dame Cathedral, and felt a thrill of wonder. Everything in my life had led to this moment. Somehow it all made sense. With every breath I was proving there was life beyond injury. I wasn't just surviving, I really was thriving – and my message to you is that perseverance can truly pay off.

My experiences were expanding rapidly. I was living way beyond my expectations –and I knew that I could keep being ambitious, could keep wanting success and going for it.

I want all you guys to know that you can break through the challenges life throws at all of us. OK, they might be different obstacles, but it doesn't mean they aren't important. But know this: if I can get where I've got, then so can you. I have never hidden my injury away. It's nothing to be ashamed of; it's just a bad card that life dealt me. Why would I feel shame for that?

So I cope with it in the same way I've always faced up to things: by putting on a hot-pink lip, by fake-tanning, by straightening my highlighted hair and by looking the very best I can. It gives me the confidence to blast through any preconceived ideas from people about how a wheelchair user should be.

I see myself as a proud, strong woman. I'm not afraid to make an impact, to raise a few eyebrows. I guess people stared at me in Paris; wherever I go I see people's gaze slide towards me then quickly away, but that's OK. I accept I'll always look different to able-bodied people, but I play this difference up now. I celebrate it – and you can, too, by finding out what makes *you* stand out from the crowd.

We headed from the bridge to the Eiffel Tower, posing for photos together in its shadow. We spent the rest of the day searching for the Champs-Élysées, making a pit stop at the Plaza Athénée hotel for lunch and a cocktail. Mike had the most expensive sandwich ever. It cost 40 euros! My Cosmopolitan cocktail was an eye-watering 29 euros, but it was worth every cent as we thoroughly enjoyed sitting on the hotel's little terrace with our food and drinks, basking in the Paris sunshine.

After lunch we had a little mooch in the designer boutiques, from Chanel to Gucci, but I was a very good girl and didn't buy anything, even though it would've been lovely to say I'd bought a designer handbag from Paris!

Arriving in the Champs-Élysées, we wandered round some shops, grabbed a coffee in an espresso bar and went to the most amazing beauty store on earth – Sephora. Why oh why doesn't the UK have one?! I did a bit of damage on my credit card but hey, you only live once!

Hours drifted by, and suddenly it was evening and we were hungry again. As our stomachs rumbled, we found another medical-themed restaurant called Drugstore Steakhouse, close to the Arc de Triomphe. Weird but true! Inside was a cool bar and a large glass window so we could watch passers-by as we sipped yet more cocktails.

I ordered salmon in a creamy sauce with mashed potato, and Mike went for an artisan burger and fries.

The next morning was our last, and we checked out before heading off for breakfast in a nearby restaurant, then getting a cab to Sacré-Coeur.

Unfortunately there was no wheelchair access that day as it was closed, but we got to drink in all the street artists and the clamour of tourists and locals. I felt so alive amid it all, and I felt so thankful to Mike for taking me there.

It was only when we were speeding through the French countryside on our train journey home that I reflected over where my life had got to. I was like any other woman in a relationship – this trip wasn't about my disability, we were just living. I was finding a way past my struggles, discovering ways to enjoy myself and working around my restrictions. I think everyone can learn from that; it's about looking beyond the immediate obstacles and learning to take pleasure from the things you *can* do. And you might just be surprised at what is possible.

18

Bombshell

Making an Impression

'You are amazing. You deserve a fantastic life!'

'Bloody hell, you're shaking! Are you still hung-over?' I peered into Mike's eyes. 'They don't seem *too* bloodshot!'

'I'm fine, I'm totally fine, though that's probably it – yeah, I did have a few too many drinks last night,' Mike replied, wiping sweat from his brow. I didn't know it, but Mike's shakes were from nerves. He had a huge surprise in store for me.

It was Christmas Day 2014. Mum, Michael, Eden, Mike and me were celebrating together. We'd opened all our gifts, and Mum and Michael were getting ready to start preparing the roast dinner, when Mike suddenly said, 'There's another gift for you. It's a special one from me.'

He held out his hand. In it was a square present, wrapped

in classic Mike style (messy!), that minutes earlier had been sitting on the arm of a chair in our bedroom. Even so, I was desperate to go and put my make-up on. I didn't feel properly ready until I'd got my routine under way.

'Thanks, babe, though can it wait? I really want to put my Christmas make-up on.' I replied, blowing him a kiss.

'Erm, no, actually, it can't wait,' he stuttered, clearly looking nervous now.

'You OK? God, you must've put it away last night, you look green!' I shouted as I wheeled myself off into our bedroom. I wasn't concerned, because Mike clearly had a hangover, and that was totally his fault, right?

He followed me into the room. 'Come here, Jordan. Let me unwrap this last gift, then you're free to get ready.'

I mock-sighed, 'Go on, then!' as if it was a huge drag having to open yet more presents from my man. He was always so generous with me.

The paper fell off and revealed a photobook.

'Aw, it's like, so pretty . . .' I said as I used my clenched fist to flick through the pages. Mike had collected the best photos of us together over the years and made a book from them.

'This is sooo romantic, babe.' Then, just as I was thinking *this is so sweet*, I paused. I had got to the page with our Paris photos, and there was one of us kissing on Love Lock Bridge, but Mike had handwritten underneath *I'd love to have done it here*, and then on the next page he'd written, *but I'll have to settle for here instead*, alongside a picture of our front room. He had been rummaging in his pocket for something as I turned the last page. What on earth was he up to?

'I don't get it,' I said, looking up expectantly, hoping I wasn't being completely thick, expecting Mike to smile back at me, but he wasn't standing up at all. He had sunk down onto one knee, bedside my dressing table, and was gazing at me intently so I could look straight into his eyes. He was holding out a small ring box.

I gasped.

Could this be it? Could this be what I'd hoped for in Paris?

I didn't have to wait long for an answer.

Mike simply said: 'Will you marry me?'

'Oh my God, are you sure?' I said breathlessly. I couldn't believe he was doing it for real.

His hands trembling, he took out the most perfect diamond ring. It was a diamond cluster ring – one diamond closely encircled by lots of smaller diamonds, with more of them lining the band as well. I like a bit of bling, and this was definitely a bling-tastic ring!

'Of course I'm sure!' he croaked.

I laughed. 'Then yes, I'd love to marry you!'

We hugged. I could feel his body judder. It was probably the relief after doing something so dramatic. He's not normally into big gestures like that!

Mike had already shown his love for me on so many occasions. When he faced the possibility of being posted to Dubai with the RAF earlier in the year, he immediately gave his year notice period and stayed with me, meaning he would be looking for new employment in 2015. He hadn't wanted to leave me. I thought that was the most romantic thing someone could ever do for me – apparently I was wrong!

When Mike didn't propose in Paris, I thought, *Oh well, perhaps he'll never do it*, and I was fine about it. I would never have wanted to push him into anything. If he was going to do it, then I wanted it to be something he wanted too. So when he did actually go down on one knee it was like a bombshell, a fairy-tale ending, a new beginning to the rest of my life. Not all bombshells are good ones – I should know – but this one was the best ever.

When life does pull a showstopper on you, circumstances might call for a dramatic make-up look to match.

In honour of bombshells of all descriptions, I created my 'bombshell' look to take you into new realms of evening glamour. This look is for the big night out, the red carpet or the film premiere. It's high-octane seduction – and should be used with caution!

To create the look, I start with a primer. It makes my skin feel really fresh. I then use foundation, smoothing it down my neck if I'm feeling a bit pasty!

Using a silk-finish brush, I apply the foundation, then brush my brows with a spooly, with which I work in the brow pomade to create my signature arched look – first using my small, angled brush to apply it. I draw a line from the front of my brow up to the arch and down towards the tail, then I fill in the middle. With whatever's left on the brush, I turn the brush to the side and apply it to the front of the brow to give a natural look. I like to make the front a little lighter, then blend into the more defined part of my brow.

I conceal with a precision brush the areas I always high-light, covering the dark circles under my eyes, popping it on my eyelids as a base for the eyeshadow and painting it in the middle of my forehead, down the centre of my nose, on the cupid's bow and my chin. Then I blend it all in, and tap with my beauty blender to make it sheer. This is when I start using colour shades: applying a yellow and a white shade to use under my eyes.

To contour, I use a darker shade from the top of my ear down towards the corner of my mouth, blending upward (never downward!). Then I use a golden shade on the top of my forehead, around the sides of my face and a little bit on top of the contour and the bottom of my chin. Then I blend again with a clean brush.

For highlight, I blend along the top of my cheekbones, in the centre of my forehead, the centre of my nose and my cupid's bow.

I then finish the cheeks with some blush.

Using the warm colours from an eyeshadow palette, I use a warm brown first, applying it with a tapered blending brush, first shading the upper crease and using a little bit on my brow bone. Then I work in a darker warm brown, running that through the crease and blending it all. Blend, blend, blend!

A cool-tone brown is next, on a wide and flat blending brush. I pop that through the crease so it's a bit deeper and darker. Using the bigger brush, with no extra product, I blend that out to avoid harsh lines. Then I use a metallic plum shade on a round-edged brush and pack that onto the base of the lid. At this point it all falls onto my nose! I forget that every time – I should sometimes do my base as the last stage, as you can get a lot of fallout from the eye make-up, depending on what shadows you use. Then I work in a deep plum shade, running that through the outer crease halfway up my brow bone.

In the inner corner of my eyes, I use a highlight shade which glistens. Next it's time for liquid eyeliner. I wing it out, making it really dramatic. With the sultry bombshell look, you can really go for it and make the wings as large as you like.

Grabbing a warm brown eyeshadow, I run it on my lower lash line, going as low as I want. The lower the better, as it makes it more sexy!

Getting the plum shade, I put a little bit of that on the

outer corner to deepen it up a bit. I use a pencil liner to draw onto my waterline. Last but not least, I use a big, voluminous mascara, but with this look I like to really glam it up with false eyelashes as well.

Finally I use a pink lipstick, then I run a small amount of gloss across my lips, making them super-pouty and sexy!

My bombshell look is my reminder that life always has the potential to be amazing, and that we are all worth having a fantastic life and looking like a superstar.

Meanwhile my online presence was going from strength to strength. My belief in myself was growing, and my reach with my blog and channel was growing too. I wouldn't let anyone tell me I couldn't succeed online. I saw any bad comments as jealousy or insecurity. I do sometimes get negative comments on my site, but I don't let them get me down. I choose to believe I am beautiful inside, which radiates to my outside. I want to spread positive energy, and I really want you to know that we are all amazing beings on this planet. We're so lucky to be here.

My bombshell look is a celebration of that. It's a big shout-out to the universe that we are all gorgeous, and that we can be even more gorgeous if we choose to. We are made up of the same minerals as the stars – I heard that in a meditation. Wow, that's *incredible* if you think about it. That means we're all stars! It's all about recognising what you like, and being who you want to be. You're unique, and you don't need to be anyone else.

I started January 2015 in a really positive way. I felt so amazing, being engaged to Mike, and seeing my vlogs getting more views and more subscribers to my YouTube channel and more readers on my blog, *Jordan's Beautiful Life*.

I did an online vlog about not comparing yourself to others, and that's a message really close to my heart. I tell my followers that your time will come, and you will achieve what you want to achieve by believing in your own positive intentions. I guess I had realised by then that by surrounding myself with happy people, with believing I would do well on YouTube, would and could work for me, like the Law of Attraction. It would increase the positive energy around me – and it seemed that all that meditation and uplifting thinking was definitely working!

I guess I should mention something about making mistakes. That's a biggie, isn't it? We *all* make mistakes. We're *all* human. It's pointless comparing yourself and your achievements to others, because we all have different challenges and goals. Even if someone is doing something similar to you, you have to follow your own heart.

I want to do really well with my blog and my channel. I'm striving to show you guys my make-up skills, and I started from scratch, moving from someone who couldn't hold a brush to someone confident enough in herself to show you my tutorials.

Strive to be who you want to be, and don't let anyone get in your way, especially you!

My expanding self-belief was working. All of my vlogs were getting views in the thousands. This was also the year that brands started coming to me (I know, right!) to review their products in my vlogs. Just a word upfront: I always say if I'm being sponsored to review a brand, and I would only ever review something I liked or felt a connection with. I always want my videos to feel authentic, so it makes sense that I only do the work I love. That way, you will know that I'm sincere and you can trust what I say.

One of the first products was a curling wand. My vlog on this was called 'How to get Glam Voluminous Curls', and the review formed the basis of my first-ever hair tutorial. I got really dressed up for that one, with a shimmery blue strappy top and gorgeous wavy hair. My carer Fiona worked her magic on my tresses. Fiona is always so amazing at doing my hair; it's like having a personal hairdresser. I don't need to tell you too much about it, but it marked the next level of my success as a vlogger.

Things felt like they were flying. That video has been viewed more than 26,000 times and I just couldn't believe it. That sounded like so many views to me! I had no idea that, very soon, things would go stratospheric. All my dreams of going big and being successful were about to come true. I say that not to boast, but to *inspire* you. If I can achieve what I was about to, and what I had achieved by then, in

October 2015, then you too can do anything you set your mind to.

If no one else is telling you you're amazing, tell yourself – really believe it. That self-belief can take you places.

19

Radiance

Going Viral

'If you believe, you will achieve.'

What's wrong with your hands?
Why don't your hands work?
Why are your hands stuck together?

Messages like these from my subscribers had increased rapidly over the past year or so. Even though I'd said ages before that my hands didn't work because of my injury, somehow it hadn't got through to people. I guess all my new followers hadn't watched my vlogs from five years ago; or perhaps I made so little mention about my wheelchair or my quadriplegia that they hadn't cottoned on. Either way, I realised I had to do, or say, something. Answering those questions had been bothering me. I didn't want to repeat old posts, but I did want to tell people my story.

On 24 August 2015, I woke up suddenly. The sun was streaming into my room. I instantly knew what I was going to do that day; what kind of video I was going to make. Inspiration had hit me, and I knew in my gut that it was going to be special.

I said to my morning carer, 'Carla, people keep asking me about my hands, why they don't work.

'I'm going to make a video today that will be different to the rest. I'm going to reveal my whole story, and show my wheelchair and my hands. I want this one to be really professional.' Carla and I are friends as well as carer and patient, and so I often chatted to her about my vlogs.

'That sounds brilliant, Jordan, you should absolutely go for it. What have you got to lose?' she replied.

I smiled to her as she transferred me out of bed and placed me carefully into my chair, making sure my body was straight and aligned correctly to stop any soreness developing later.

'It'll be cool to be focused and film it really well. So should I pay for a professional cameraman, or should I try it myself?' I mused.

'You know what? I think I'll have a go on my own. I can always get someone in if I don't like the result.'

'Go girl!' said Carla in a mock-American accent, and we both giggled. 'I'll just get your breakfast ready while you plan out your mega-stardom,' she added, winking at me as she left my room.

Once I was ready, I asked Carla to set up my camera and make sure the lighting was right. I'd finally splashed out on a proper camera to replace using my webcam.

It's odd; I didn't plan out the video. Somehow it seemed to work organically. Usually I talked straight to my camera in a flow of consciousness. I would sometimes write out what I wanted to say on my phone and read that out, but mostly I liked to be natural and speak from my heart.

This time I decided to film myself first, then do a voice-over. It was a new departure, and I felt quite nervous and excited during the set-up. I had the camera angled down onto my lap, putting my hands in focus. They filled the screen. That felt quite scary. What if people reacted with disgust? It felt like a big risk, exposing myself like that.

Then Carla held the camera and filmed me from behind, sitting at my vanity table in my wheelchair. Then I filmed myself wearing no make-up at all, showing the world how difficult it had been to try and open a mascara wand, or hold the applicator close to my eye. I showed people my struggles, my upset and my emotions. It was a revelation. I didn't hide my difficulties with the applicators (I usually edited those bits out); this time I really celebrated it. I showed people what it was like to be me, and how hard it was to do something as simple as put make up on my face.

For the first time, people could see what I'd been through to get to where I was. My story really hit home. I created a window into my world, a mirror where I was reflected, showing the truth that lay behind my smiling face in my videos. Perhaps it was because it was truly authentic, or because I showed the struggles under the gloss and the frustrations beneath the positive thinking, that it became such an overnight online sensation.

Looking back at the video, I feel so moved at the journey I've been on, and how I've finally shared it properly with you guys out there. And you loved it. I mean, really loved it.

In my vlog I said: 'Most of the time I upload my videos I have questions about my hands.

'Truth is, I can't move them, open them or close them. It's all because ten years ago I became a tetraplegic after a car accident. So to be able to do my make-up well enough to show you guys is a massive achievement for me.

'This is how it used to be for me. I was depressed. For years I would struggle; my arms were weak. And I didn't know how I could use my what seemed to be useless hands. I wanted the world still to see Jordan, even though I became a tetraplegic.

'I lost a lot, and I didn't want to lose my identity too. Being the girl in the wheelchair wasn't my plan, so I didn't want people to see just the chair. It was so hard, but the perseverance was so worth it in the end. If only I'd known back then.

'Tears would fall. Frustration would drive me crazy. I wouldn't leave the house because I would drop mascara down my face and down my clothes. And I would wonder,

Why me? Why me?? But I persevered, and I'm happy at how my useless hands help me enhance my face each day. It's insane how much we grow with the challenges we face.

'Each day I learn more. Each day my blending improves, and each day my eyeliner becomes less of a challenge, even though there are still those days when I think, *aargh!*

'There are so many struggles in my life. I mean, I can't dress myself or do my own hair, so to be able to do my own make-up is my thing.

'In this video I show you things I would normally edit out, like how I use my mouth to help me with my brushes. It may be weird, but it's my way.

'Like contouring and highlighting teaches us, where there is darkness there is always light. That is the same with life. No matter what hardship you are going through, remember that even in the darkest times there is always a light shining brighter.

'I don't know what you're going through right now. But know that each day is worth living. Know that you're worth so much. Know that you're amazing.

'I have many challenges right now; my injury is just one of them, but I know that life *will* get better.

'My hands haven't been able to move in ten years, but I've taught myself a new way of doing my make-up. So if something is standing in your way, maybe it means trying a different way. Explore your options. The obvious route may not always be the route for you.

'I hope you can apply this video to your life somehow, and that it inspires you, no matter what your situation. You guys inspire me every day, so I hope this is a little way of saying thank you. Showing the vulnerable you isn't always easy, but know you are amazing, and you are *so* beautiful, no matter what. Just always be yourself and believe in yourself.

'What prompted me to do this video was how people would leave comments on my videos about my hands, and, you know, people on social media sometimes say things without thinking, and sometimes it hurts.

'So next time you ask someone a sensitive question or leave a negative comment, think, just think, about how it might affect their day.

'Always spread positivity and be kind. Life is far too short to waste it with negativity. So I hope you have a beautiful day. Thank you so much for watching.

'Get out there in the world and push yourself. We only have one life, so love the life you live.'

I guess I could've reacted badly to people leaving negative comments about my hands, and the fact that they didn't work, but I don't believe that is ever the way forward. Two negatives don't make a positive! I also wanted to say something about how we use social media, and how we behave on it. Sometimes people don't think we're real, just because we're in front of a camera. But we are. We have hearts and minds just like you! So when someone says something mean or upsetting, it can be hurtful. I guess what I'm trying to say is be kind online. The person you're commenting on is just like you, except they've been brave enough to share their story, skills or talent on digital media.

Don't slate us for the sake of it. By all means leave constructive criticism. It's healthy to say what you like and don't like, and it's good for YouTubers like myself to get honest feedback: it helps us improve our vlogs and respond to people out there. But please don't use Twitter, YouTube, Facebook or any of the other sites just to bring people down. You wouldn't like it if we did it to you!

Online bullying is a huge issue. We read about teenagers getting harassed to death on sites almost every week. Bullying can have tragic effects on people's lives – and the lives of their families. I learnt from the time when I was ganged up on, that the more energy and attention I gave it, the more stressed and unhappy I felt, so I decided to ignore it and carry on with my life as best I could. It worked. The bullies eventually got bored of me and I made loads of new friends by being myself and being friendly. By leaving nasty comments online you could unwittingly be bullying someone, so if that happens just delete and find someone you'd rather watch instead.

OK, lecture over!

After I made the video, I talked to my friend and fellow YouTuber TashieTinks about what to call it. I suggested

'My Beautiful Struggle', and she loved it. It summed up everything about me: my difficulties, my journey and my passion.

When I'd finished it I felt very emotional – I think I even cried a bit! It was like seeing someone else's life, and for a second I just thought, wow, I've been so brave! I know that sounds silly, but it was a special moment.

I edited it and added my voice-over. I wrote what I wanted to say in one go. I didn't need to edit or change the words because they were all true. I was showing the world the real me. I did it all on my laptop. No fancy film crew; no practice run. I just got on and did it myself.

The next day, on 25 August 2015, I published it on my YouTube channel. I knew I'd made something unique, something utterly from my heart and totally sincere.

I spent the day tweeting it from my Twitter account @JordanBone1. I wanted to get it out to the world because I knew it was worth seeing. My breakthrough moment that day was when mega-successful YouTuber Zoella retweeted my video to her millions of followers. I'm assuming you know who Zoella is – if not, she's a fashion and beauty vlogger from Brighton (real name Zoe Suggs). Her partner is Alfie Deyes (known on YouTube as PointlessBlog), and she started on YouTube way back in 2009. She even has her own range of products called Zoella Beauty, so you can imagine how thrilled I was when she noticed me. It felt incredible!

By the end of the day 50,000 people had viewed my video.

Yep, you read that right, fifty thousand people! I felt it could go big, but I never expected it to go viral.

'Why don't you put it on Facebook?' suggested Mike the next evening. We were sitting at the dining table, watching the number of my subscribers go up by the minute on my laptop.

'D'you think it'd work on that site?' I asked. At that time I was more into my YouTube stuff than Facebook, but Mike really saw the opportunity.

'Loads of celebs look at Facebook and share stuff. It might go really massive. It's worth giving it a go,' he said, placing a bowl of pasta in front of me. I clicked my laptop shut and studied him.

'Since when did you know so much about social media?' I quipped.

'Er, since I went into business myself!' he laughed, seemingly outraged.

'Oh yeah, sorry, babe. Great idea, I'll upload it after we've eaten,' I replied, giving him a cheeky grin.

When Mike left the RAF he was a Senior Aircraftman, but he wanted to launch his own personal fitness and nutrition site. He went on to set up MH Fitness & Nutrition (his name is Mike Harrison).

It also meant that Mike could be around more to support me, and help out. Every night he cooked dinner and we'd grab a few precious moments to discuss our day before we spent the evening chilling in front of the TV. Well, that's what we used to do together. Those days, we were both so obsessed with making a success of what we were doing, we were more likely to be on our laptops, or on the phone!

That evening I put the video on Facebook, and that's when things went crazy. Celebrities such as Ashton Kutcher and Nicki Minaj shared it. The magazine *Cosmopolitan* (US edition) also shared it on their website, and all of a sudden everyone seemed to be sharing it. It was on the websites of every magazine I'd ever heard of, and by the end of the next day it had had a million views.

I couldn't believe it. It was the success I'd longed for, but it felt like a dream. On Facebook the numbers soared to 17 million views to date. I don't even understand numbers that big! As you know, maths was never my strong point! My simple video, shot in one day and edited in one take, had gone into orbit.

It has now been viewed almost six million times on You-Tube. It's insane to think that so many people have seen my video. Something about it caught people's imaginations. Perhaps they could feel it was my truth. Again I'd turned round the negative responses and made them into a positive experience.

That year, 2015, became the year I hit TV on the back of my video's success. In September I appeared on ITV's *Lorraine*. We had met at an Avon event, and she was so lovely.

I messaged her on Twitter, never expecting her to get back to me. She had shared my video, and so I asked her if ITV would be interested in having me on her show. She replied saying she'd already spoken to her producer about me!

I was so nervous beforehand, thinking I'd say something stupid on live TV! But then my adrenalin kicked in and I felt instantly at ease and just chatted away with Lorraine. I actually enjoyed it! I guess by that time I was used to speaking in front of a camera.

Then I was invited to be in the audience of ITV's *Inspiring People* in October, fronted by Lorraine. The show celebrated people who had overcome unbelievable obstacles in their lives. I felt so honoured to be invited, and Lorraine even came and chatted to me on air.

I'd been really nervous about doing those programmes, but I soon learnt the maxim that you only regret the things you didn't do, and the opportunities you didn't take.

I got to speak on an American show called *Doctors*. I talked on the phone, and in the background I could hear the audience whooping, saying 'yeah!' and being really over the top. That was hilarious. Such a difference compared to British audiences, which are much more reserved.

At this point I decided I needed a manager; I didn't understand about licensing my videos and other industry know-how, so I contacted a creative agency called Red Hare that represents digital influencers. Jonathan, the guy who runs it, got straight back to me. He came to see me in King's Lynn and I signed a contract that day. I haven't looked back since!

Every step forward for me is worth appreciating. Once you begin to take stock of the good stuff, it's funny how moments seem to build up into something bigger. My view is that every victory, every bit of recognition, big or small, is important to note. And that year was full of little victories.

Kylie Jenner shared one of my pictures of her hair extensions on Instagram, getting more than 477,000 likes! I thought that was the height of fame, showing I had no idea how big my videos would go!

I had also met Katie Piper (she's so awesome, she's my inspiration) around the same time, spring 2015, at the Ideal Home Show. Katie and I fronted a live chat on stage. It was so exciting, such a great opportunity. I loved every minute of it, from the hotel the night before, to having my hair and make-up done backstage, to seeing the audience hanging on my every word. I felt I was making a difference.

Katie told the crowd: 'I feel like I know her [me] because of being online!' I spoke about showing the world who I was through my make-up, and how I wouldn't let my disability shape my identity. My tip for building confidence was meditation, because it makes me feel happier, and that in turn makes me more confident. Katie was amazing. She was a fashion and beauty ambassador for the show, and she shared with the audience that years ago she would never have thought she could represent beauty. I told the crowds that beauty was about empowering ourselves, and for me that was with dressing up and make-up, but for you it could be anything. As Katie said, looks are important. When she was in hospital she said that she'd had her toes painted and that made her feel better. It's such a simple way of lifting your spirits.

Katie asked me to give the audience a quote to sum up a way of being more positive.

'If you believe, you will achieve! Because if you don't believe in yourself, who will?' I answered.

'That is going to be my mantra!' Katie said to the crowd as the audience clapped. It was such a great day. I'm so lucky to get to do so many varied and interesting things, and that people want to hear about my journey.

Going viral changed everything. This is what I'd wanted to happen so badly; succeeding in what I love and making a difference to other people's lives. My blog, *Jordan's Beautiful Life*, had become a bigger success than I ever imagined; my channel on YouTube has 183,000 subscribers to date (and counting).

With hard work and determination, I had stood out from the crowd. I had smashed through life's challenges and been reborn like a phoenix from the ashes.

I prove daily that the impossible can become the possible. I moved from injury into radiance. I believe beauty is as much about an inner energy as it is about outer looks. By projecting positive thoughts and actions, I allowed my inner radiant self to shine through, shattering perceptions about paralysis in the process.

Yet my message is so simple: 'Believe in who you are. Believe in yourself, and you will achieve.' Let your radiance shine through. You are so beautiful.

20

Reflection

Living with Passion

'You have one life, live it – with the full force of your desire.'

'Oh my God, oh my *God*!' I shrieked. Mum, Michael, Eden and Michael and me were sat in the lounge. I was looking at my emails.

'What's the matter, Jordan, are you OK?' Mum started.

'Yes! Mum, you won't believe it, I can't believe it!' I said, staring with wide eyes at my computer screen.

'Tell me, sugar, or I'll implode!' Mum laughed. I turned to her, speaking uncharacteristically slowly.

'We've. Been. Invited. To . . . New York City!!' I gushed. It was literally a dream come true. An all-expenses-paid trip to the Big Apple as the guest of one of my favourite brands, Urban Decay.

'New York! Oh my God, that's amazing. When are you

going? Is Mike coming too? Do you need carers? I can come if you need me. What if I can't get time off work, if it's during term time?' (Mum is a teaching assistant.)

'Mum, you're worse than me. You need to calm down!' I giggled.

'Jane, you should definitely go with Jordan. It's the trip of a lifetime for her career,' interjected Michael, a huge grin on his kind face.

'I am definitely coming, I don't care what else is going on. NYC . . .' whistled Mike. He was well up for it!

'OK, listen to this: I got an email from Urban Decay, that brand that I really love?' Everyone but Mum shrugged, but I continued anyway.

'They sent me an email saying, *Do you want to go on a press trip?* So of course, I replied, *Yes! But where to?*'

'Well, I scrolled down the email and saw my invitation. It said New York City! Oh my God! It's to help promote the launch of the Urban Decay X Gwen Stefani Spring Collection!' I was crying by now, tears streaming down my face. Thank goodness for waterproof mascara!

Mike whooped. Everyone was so excited. I watched them all surrounding me with their smiles through a mist of tears. I had been to New York for my twenty-first birthday, but this was different. This was because a brand wanted me to go for them. Amazing!

Out of everything, this felt like the moment I'd really made it. It brought everything back to me – all my hopes and dreams seemed to merge. I felt like I'd done something right. It felt like a validation of everything I'd worked for: every vlog, every motivational speech, every appearance. I knew in that moment that I was achieving, despite my challenges.

I wished I could have told that fifteen-year-old girl, lying on that hospital bed with the metal halo screwed into her skull, that one day she would be flown Upper Class to one of the best cities in the world. I know she wouldn't have believed it. For a while, the world looked so bleak to her.

When I got the news, I felt so proud of who I had become. I was a success. I had found motivation and purpose when I had felt like all hope was gone.

As you can tell, the trip to New York meant so much more to me than a free press trip. It became the symbol of my re-emergence. It meant people were taking me seriously, and that I had something to give to the world. I was on the right track at last.

'So when are you going?

'The trip is on 6 January, only a few weeks away! I cannot wait! I'll email and double-check how many people I can take with me as carers too. I hope you can get time off, Mum!'

Jo and Jen, the PR girls at Urban Decay, were great. They emailed back straight away to say that I could bring Mum and Mike as my carers – and that they too would travel Upper Class with Virgin. Luckily Mum's school were great about giving her a couple of days off to come.

Everything was set. When the day arrived to leave, I was so hyped up. I'd been awake since 2 a.m., half excited and half worried about the travelling. A taxi picked us all up and took us to Heathrow Airport, the only hitch being that, on arrival at the Upper Class wing, the cab driver spoke over the intercom saying he was carrying 'Gordon Bone'! It really made me laugh. We were waved through, and for the first time I really felt like a celebrity. It was so cool!

In the Upper Class lounge I had a big bowl of chia seed porridge, Mike had a breakfast burger while Mum chose eggs royale with smoked salmon. The waiters brought us pastries and plenty of coffee. Then afterwards I *had* to go and explore.

The lounge was space-age cool with a long trendy bar, smart staff and even a hairdressing suite. This was a whole new experience for me. I don't travel that much, and when I do, it's never that swanky. Totally awesome!

I was living the dream.

'Wow, look, Jordan, we've got our own booths!' said Mum, delighted, as we boarded the plane.

'Yeah, and we're opposite each other – cool. Look, we've got movies, and a glass of champagne!' I squealed. I really think I did squeal out of happiness!

Once inside the aircraft, we found our seriously fancy seats and settled in. We were served a yummy afternoon tea with cakes, sandwiches and cups of tea in beautiful porcelain.

'This is nothing like travelling economy!' Mum said.

'I'll never be able to fly economy again after this!' I laughed. 'It's all right, isn't it?' I looked around. The booths had strips of pink lights on them. The design was incredible, really smart.

We were met in New York by a chauffeur-driven car, which took us down the highway. Seeing the spires and towers of NYC getting closer was just fantastic. Seriously, I was being treated like a Hollywood celeb! We were dropped at the Mercer Hotel, which was beautiful, really classy with expensive muted decor and high ceilings. Our room had the biggest mirror in the world, and a bathroom with marble floors. Apparently New York hotel rooms always have tiny rooms – I guess the cost of everything is just so high, but our room was enormous. Mike filmed it for my NYC vlog, and the video really didn't do it justice.

On the coffee table in our room was a handwritten note saying, *Dear Jordan, Welcome to the Mercer! Have a great stay with us, and let us know if you need anything. Warm Regards, Gilles* (He was the managing director!)

It felt so wonderful to be treated like this; it couldn't have been a better start to the trip! We had less than an hour to change and get ready, as we were due out at the Rockefeller Center. Travelling through the city, we filmed the sights.

'Look, Jordan, it's Macy's, you'll like that,' said Mike, holding the camera steady as the car drove slowly through the intensity of the traffic, the lights and the soaring buildings.

'Oh, there's Radio City Music Hall. That's famous, isn't it? It's just so magical,' I answered, gazing out of the window.

We took the elevator to the Top of the Rock observation deck at the Rockefeller Center. The city was laid out beneath us, twinkling with a trillion Christmas lights. It was breathtaking, truly an unbelievable experience. I sat there and just gazed out, my heart and spirit soaring. Literally, if I'd have died that night I would've been happy. It felt like the pinnacle of what I had been working towards, and we'd only just arrived!

Wheeling around the city, sightseeing, we passed through tree-lined streets, the individual branches of the trees laced with lights making them look strangely translucent. With my spirits so high, it all felt surreal and wondrous.

We had dinner at Buddakan, the magnificent Asian restaurant in Chelsea Market, which was in the *Sex and the City* movie. That was amazing. The food was great, but I was more excited about being anywhere that *SITC* was filmed! We were shattered, though, so we headed back to the hotel for a bath and some sleep. We were only there for two nights, so we wanted to make the most of our time in New York. I was really tired, but it was the most special time ever and I didn't want to miss a minute.

I felt so much happiness bubbling up inside me. I didn't

care that I was exhausted! I felt like I'd won a 'life' competition. I was there for work, to promote the brand, but I was so grateful they'd chosen me. I never thought that anything like that trip would ever happen to me. I saw other vloggers go on trips, and thought it would be so cool.

The next day, we got up early and headed out to do a boat trip on the Hudson River, taking in the sights. It was a beautiful sunny winter's day, but cold. I had to wear thermals under my usual black leggings! The highlight was passing by the Statue of Liberty. Seeing her blew me away. What a symbol to be inspired by. She has encouraged generations of Americans, people arriving at the docks full of hope to live the American Dream. How many people must've been spurred on to live the best life they could by seeing her?

That's why I wanted to share my inspirational story with you guys. If just one of you goes out there and changes your thinking or your attitude, then that means the world to me.

Of course, any trip to New York with me in it wouldn't be complete without doing some serious shopping! I wanted to get to Sephora, the best make-up store ever and my idea of complete heaven; Victoria's Secret (of course) and CVS (a drugstore selling make-up).

That night was the launch of the Urban Decay collaboration with US singer Gwen Stefani (though sadly she wasn't there for it). I had a hairdresser come to my room. Luxury! Then I did my own make-up: a bombshell look for night with smoky, dark eyes courtesy of my Urban Decay palette, of course. My hair was big and bouncy, really swishy, just right for a night out in NYC, and I wore a River Island top, sparkly leggings, my Chanel bag and glittery Louboutin heels that never fail me.

I was whisked to the event, held in a cool bar. The whole place was lit with neon pink light, there was a brilliant band and I got to meet lots of American YouTubers. Wende, the founder, and I got chatting. She was really nice, and she told me she lived in the OC (Orange County), so I told her how much I had always wanted to go there! I also met one of Madonna's make-up artists.

Not bad for a girl from King's Lynn!

Madonna is such a big influence on millions of people; she is so successful and strong. It felt great to meet someone who helped create her look.

We drove through Times Square, to get back to the hotel. Amazing!

Our last morning was spent munching on blueberry pancakes for breakfast, then a trip to Carlo's Bakery, where we couldn't choose between the cakes, they all looked so delicious.

New York was so much fun. I'm just so lucky I was asked to go. I was given a goody bag filled with all of the UDXGWEN products, which made it feel like Christmas all over again. The Gwen Collection consisted of an eyeshadow palette, a blush palette, a brow box, lip liners and lipsticks. When I think of Gwen I always think 'lipstick', so I did a blog about the lipsticks and lip liners. The packaging of the lip products had a 1920s art deco vibe with a black and gold print, which I loved!

Each of the lip liners was given the same name as the lipsticks, so they were a match made in heaven. This made it so easy to know which pair to buy, but hey, obviously there are *no* rules when it comes to make-up (within reason!), so you could use any liner with the lipstick you desired, with names such as Plaid, Rock Steady and Firebird. Great names!

A tip for making your lipstick last longer is to not only line your lips but fill them in completely with the lip liner before applying the lipstick. Just thought I'd add that!

The year went from amazing to incredible for me.

In April 2016, Mike and I moved into our new home, which we'd built from scratch with the help of my stepfather Michael over the preceding two years. Obviously everything had to be created to fit my lifestyle and my wheelchair, but it was such a pleasure to choose the plans, the flooring, the style and feel of our house. The house was built in Mum's back garden, and we needed planning permission to go ahead; luckily that was granted, as it's only one storey so it doesn't obstruct any views. And now I have my mum close by for support too!

We built a bungalow-style property, with vintage floorboards, stylish Scandinavian wooden feature walls and high ceilings. I loved it. It is mine and Mike's first real home together – and it was such a labour of love to complete. We even decided to postpone our wedding until it was finished. I prefer to concentrate on one thing at a time, and do each thing as well as I can. I'm a bit of a perfectionist. I aim high, in a positive way. So now it's complete, I guess I can get the wedding magazines back out again, eh, girls?

The journey might have been stressful at times, but the end result was completely worth it.

Being able to call my new house my home was incredible. There are no restrictions here. I can get into every single room, which is a wonderful feeling in a world that isn't usually built with wheelchair users in mind. People take it for granted that their surroundings fit their abilities; it's only once you become impaired in some way that you realise the smallest adjustments make a big difference.

The first night we moved in, we had the fire going and a glass of Prosecco to celebrate. It felt strangely quiet; it felt like *our* place. I loved it.

'Shh, everyone, shh. I really want to say something.' I smiled at the friends and relatives in our new outside space.

Mike was at the new barbecue area, the veggie burgers, prawns and chicken wings sizzling, nicely throwing out their charcoal-grilled aroma. I knew everyone was hungry, and probably a little tipsy, as we'd been enjoying Prosecco.

'Hey, guys, I just really want to say a huge thank you to you all. It means so much that you are here. I really wanted today to be special. It has so many memories for me – mostly bad, let's face it – but we're turning it around and making a celebration of the anniversary of my accident, and I couldn't have done it all without you.

'I'm just so grateful. I wouldn't be here without Mum, especially; and Eden, Michael and Mike. They are my rocks. They've supported me, and, oh yes, Katie, and Sam, Grace, our friend Jackie, Fiona and Nanno,' I said, listing all the people at the barbecue, 'and so many others. You guys mean the world to me.

'Look, I'm raising my glass to you. You are all *so* amazing. We have one life, so let's live it!'

With that, everyone raised their glass of bubbly and cheered. I felt so emotional. It was 7 May 2016, eleven years since the crash. Instead of moping about, regretting the past, Mike and I had decided to host a party at our new home with all the people who had stuck by me through thick and thin.

Once the evening was dying down and we were sitting quietly together, Mike whispered in my ear: 'I'm the luckiest man in the world. I love you, Jordan; we get on so well, and you're incredibly beautiful in every way. Most of the time, I forget you're in a wheelchair! I just don't see the chair.'

'Tell me about it, babe!' I said; I was always having to remind him to pick things up for me!

'I was bricking it when I asked you to marry me, but we're as good as married anyway,' he added. 'We share everything together; I'm just so happy I met you.

'Jordan, you are just Jordan to me. I don't see paralysis or anything like that.'

And if that wasn't brilliant enough, the brand partnerships flooded in over the course of the next few months, and I even found time to raise awareness of spinal cord injuries. In February I had launched #TheJordanHandChallenge, challenging my followers to film themselves applying make-up without the use of their fingers. People could move their wrist, like me, but not fingers or thumbs! My big tip was to tape the fingers down but leave the thumb free. I cannot move my thumb, but when I move my wrist back it brings my thumb towards my finger, making it easier to hold brushes . . . but I have zero grip!

So many of you took part! My friend and fellow You-Tuber, TashieTinks, really went for it.

Thanks, guys – you all really helped people understand how difficult it is to apply make-up as a tetraplegic.

In 2016 I videoed a tutorial using only Urban Decay's summer range, then went on to film my collaboration with Mark Hill's Pick & Mix interchangeable wands, creating three different hairstyles.

Later in the year I was chosen to take part in the L'Oréal True Match campaign, with twenty-two other people selected because of their amazing or inspirational stories, matched to the twenty-three shades of foundation. I couldn't believe it when Mum, Eden and I entered Superdrug in King's Lynn and saw a huge cardboard cutout of me next to the L'Oréal counter!

I was *so* proud of that campaign, and such a lucky lady to be part of something so huge. I still cannot believe it! Dream big, guys! Is this even real life?! All I can say is, WE ARE ALL WORTH IT!

Even though I became a quadriplegic, I have always wanted the world to see Jordan, not a wheelchair, nor a disability. Through positive thinking and make-up, I have done that. I lost everything in that crash: the use of most of my body, my freedom, many friends, and I didn't want to lose my identity as well. That would have been the cruellest blow.

Being 'the girl in the wheelchair' wasn't ever my plan. It took perseverance to go beyond that, but it was worth every hardship along the way. Many times in hospital I asked, why me? There was never an answer. So I simply gave up asking that question. It never got me anywhere but into loads of self-pity, and that's never a good look! I decided to turn my terrible situation into something I could be proud of, and I think I've achieved that. My passions saw me through – my love of singing, my fascination with beauty and make-up.

I'm not saying I wouldn't want a cure for spinal cord injury. Of course I would! But I don't live my life in hope of it. Being paralysed never gets any easier, and I'd be the first to be a medical 'guinea pig' if the opportunity ever arose, but I don't wake up every day thinking about it, and that in itself is a huge achievement.

Today, I'm happy with how my useless hands help me enhance my face each day. It's incredible how much we grow with the challenges we face. Each day I learn more. Each day my blending improves, my eyeliner becomes less of a challenge. When I finish my make-up, I always take a second to check my reflection, to allow myself the tiniest amount of satisfaction in enjoying what I've achieved. It's a small thing, but I never forget where I've come from, and how far from my prognosis I've taken myself.

There are so many everyday struggles in my life. So being able to do my own make-up is my way of helping myself be better. My hands haven't moved in twelve years, yet I have taught myself a new way to apply my products. So if something is standing in your way, then find another way!

Explore your options. The obvious route may not be the one for you.

I know that you guys, all of you who have watched my vlogs and subscribed to my YouTube channel, inspire me daily. Sharing my troubles and my achievements with you is my way of saying thank you.

Don't let your struggles consume your existence. Although life may be hard, you can still reach for the stars if you believe in yourself enough. It can be so easy to give up when your life isn't going the way you had planned. But do you want to be the person who didn't try to live a great life despite a hard situation?

Prove yourself wrong and go for it. Your life can lead you

to amazing things if you believe in yourself. As I keep saying (because I want to ram it home), you deserve an amazing life, but the world doesn't owe you a living. That's why you have to pick yourself up each and every time you stumble or fail, and keep pushing yourself. One day you'll shine.

If you succeed, then great, and if you don't get to exactly where you wanted to be, then at least you tried your best. There were times in the past when I thought I didn't want to live any more, but I am *so* glad I didn't give up. Life is hard. There are *so* many things I wish I could change, but every day I try to live a great life.

I hope you do the same. For me, I take pleasure in all of my accomplishments – big and small. I make sure I appreciate every single highlight. Who can believe that big brands now ask me to do make-up demonstrations at the department stores in Oxford Street? Someone like me . . . *I* can't! It's such a privilege. I haven't even had any formal training, let alone being paralysed! And I love meeting you guys out there at these events. That's always the best part of the day. Perhaps applying make-up is the bit of self-care that you need, the little pep-up or confidence boost to face the world and improve the rest of your life.

Beauty, to me, means radiating your natural self, finding what empowers *you* and owning it. It is so much more than mere products or hairstyles. We all have our own route to feeling good, and I am here just to encourage you to find yours, whether that's make-up or not.

Obviously you guys get to see a lot of my life and hear my feelings about things, including my injury. Sharing my vulnerabilities isn't always easy. I don't know what you are going through right now, but know that you are worth so much.

I'm telling you now, but tell yourself too: you are amazing. You are so beautiful. Always spread positivity and be kind. Life is too short to waste it with negativity.

Believe in yourself. Have the courage to *be* yourself – and everything will follow. So, I hope you have a beautiful day. Get out there in the world and make your dreams your reality. We only have one life, so love the life that you live.

Sending you guys all my love, as ever,

Jordan X

Epilogue: Skincare

Final Thoughts

Your dreams only become a reality if you make them happen!

The changes in my life have been gradual; positivity comes step by step, and we build resilience with routine. I make sure I treat my thoughts with as much care as my make-up.

Routine plays a big part in my life, and my skincare routine is one of the most important parts of my morning and night-time rituals. It shapes my day, much as it prepares my skin for the make-up I wear, and replenishes it at night.

Every morning, I wash my hands and then start to cleanse. I move the product over my skin in circular motions, then polish using the muslin cloth that comes with the cleanser. I rub this, using hot water, over my face, making my skin feel clean and fresh. Once completed, I dry my face with a clean towel.

Then I use an exfoliator once a week, working it into my skin the same way I do with the cleanser, avoiding my eye area. It takes away dry skin and all those bits you want removed. I wash it off with water. Then I go in with a skin tonic spritzer, spraying it all over my face, pressing it into my skin.

Following that, I pat eye cream around my eyes and then I rub moisturiser in in upward circular motions.

Once the day is done, I reverse the routine – my make-up needs to come off so that my skin is left clean and pure.

I use facial wipes, sweeping them gently over my face and eyes. Then I cleanse and spritz again.

I feel using the products day and night makes my skin respond better to them.

In the evening I like to use some facial oil, popping two pumps onto my hands, warming it then massaging it into my skin in upward and outward motions.

I work in a night-repair eye serum, as it helps with my dark circles, then finish with a moisturiser.

These daily rituals are part of me. I find that not only does my skincare routine make my skin healthier and happier, it also gives me a chance to reflect. At the start of the day I have a few moments preparing for what's to come, running ideas for vlogs through my head, thinking of opportunities I've been offered and what to go for next.

In the evening, it helps me to wind down, take some time for myself (I never get enough of that!) and think over what

I have achieved each day. It benefits me physically, but perhaps it is even more important mentally.

Today things for me are not that much different to how they were twelve years ago. I am still confined to a wheelchair. I cannot open or close my hands. I have some movement in my wrists, and in both arms, and I need as much care as I did back then. Yet my life has turned around 360 degrees.

When negatives start to tug you down, acknowledge that feeling and then let it go. Take time to appreciate the good. People are often prone to finding flaws, and it's easy to home in on the negative situations in our lives and forget to value all of the positives. As soon as we focus on the good things, we become happier. It worked for me! Be grateful for your health, your family and anything that fulfils your life.

Life can be wonderful, if you let it. Our struggles will be there, but if we get on with our lives and appreciate the good, the positives will make the negatives seem less important. Bad things don't always disappear, but they can lose their weight. Find your own rituals to make things work.

I want the last words of my book to go to my sister Eden – bubbly, chatty, bright Eden.

The day she turned fifteen, in May 2016, was hard for me. I know she feels under pressure not to let me down, not to do what I did and risk her life, but I know she must be free to live her own life. One of the most special things that came from my accident was being as close as I am to my sister. If I'd have hung back, kissed her four-year-old face and stayed in the house for longer, thereby missing Tim and Jamie in that car, then I'd have grown up a normal teenager and left home. We would never have had the bond we have now, and in a weird way I'm so grateful for that.

I know I 'mother' Eden (sorry, Eden, that must be really annoying!), and I know Eden is always trying to 'steal' my make-up (Eden, you are so busted!) but we love each other deeply. I just want Eden to live a normal, nice life where she is free to come and go as she pleases. That, to me, is heaven.

And the driver of the car that day? I never mention him. He was a boy when it happened. I have no idea who or what he is as a man. I never think of him. I never even think badly of him. He is irrelevant to my life. I don't even hate him. If anything, the only emotion I've ever felt towards him is pity.

Disregard the unimportant influences in your life – acknowledge, let go, move forward.

Making *My Beautiful Struggle* was a turning point in my recovery. So many of you watched it, and continue to watch it. So many of you joined my YouTube family. So many of you have responded to it, and that online support has given me an extra-special boost.

I'll leave you with my final message – but it's the most important one I have for you.

Believe, and you *will* achieve. You are more beautiful, more resilient and more magnificent than you ever thought possible. Dream big, and never be scared to shine your light on the world.

Acknowledgements

Without sounding like I have just won an Oscar I'd firstly like to thank anyone that has ever believed in me. To everyone at Trapeze, especially Emma, for taking a chance and helping me share my story. To Cathryn, without your help this book wouldn't be in my readers' hands right now. To my managers, Jonathan and Kate and the entire Red Hare team, thank you for the opportunities so far. You are helping make my dreams become a reality – this book being one of them!

A massive thank you goes to anyone who has ever liked, commented and subscribed to me on my various social media platforms; you lovely people help me become successful. Without your interaction I wouldn't be anywhere, so thank you from the bottom of my heart. When you share your stories with me and sometimes tell me that I have inspired you in some small way, it lights a spark in me that wants to inspire you more, so really you inspire me. You give me purpose.

Thank you to anyone who has helped me live my life by being my personal assistant. You all know the impact you have on my everyday life so I thank the loyal and wonderful women I have had the pleasure of meeting.

To my handful of loyal friends; you are so important to me and I thank you for making me realise that when it comes to friendships quality outshines quantity every time.

To my wonderful family; Auntie Jackie, Fred, Pru, Flo, Nanno, Nanny Janice and Auntie Nicki – I thank you for being there for me and Mum during the good times but most importantly the bad times. To my beautiful Eden, you don't know how amazing you are. I am so proud to call you my sister and I am so excited to see the incredible things you do with your life. To Michael, for being the best stepdad a girl could ask for; you came into my life when I was in my late teens yet you have been such a father figure to me.

To Mum, what can I say? You are my best friend. You are just the most incredible woman, without your love and support I wouldn't be the person I am today. I know most daughters say they have the best mum in the world but I truly do because you have been both my mum and my dad. You support me in everything I do and look out for me in every way possible. At 27, I shouldn't be needing your help but you still help me without any resentment. I love you and will forever be grateful for everything you have done and continue to do for me. Who'd have thought I'd be writing a book? You always say you are proud of me but really you should be proud of yourself because you made me who I am.

To Mike, my one and only, thank you for loving me for me. I am so thankful to have found someone I can be my complete self with. I love feeling so comfortable with you, from wearing no make-up, to fully glam – you take me as I am. Thank you for joining me on this crazy rollercoaster called life, I know it can't always be easy but I am glad we are on this journey together. Thank you for everything you do. Here's to many more chapters of our story. I'm excited to see what the future holds.

And finally, a thank you has to go to those who are no longer with us but impacted my life so much: my grandma, Rose, I was so lucky to have a great grandparent like you for as long as I did. I know you would be so proud of me right now – you always were. And my Granddad John, I know you're looking down on me dancing and singing away as I do the same. I would like to hope you thought I would make something of myself and I hope you are proud.

So with all that said, let's raise a glass and celebrate life because its bloody fabulous when you think about it.

Jordan's Beauty Favourites

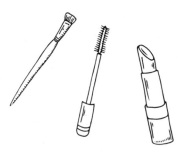

Throughout each chapter of the book, I've written about the different aspects of my life and how I relate them to elements of beauty. For anyone who is interested in the specifics of my love for make-up – which products I use and adore, how I apply them and when I use them – I've compiled the information below.

PRIMER

My favourite primer at the moment is the **Too Faced Hangover Replenishing Face Primer**. It's really hydrating, and I like it because my skin always feels silky-smooth after applying it. It's a great base for my foundation and for my skin as it sometimes feels dry.

I do have some other top picks too. For instance, the

Becca Backlight Priming Filter is great for giving your skin even more of a glow. I also like to smooth over some **Make Up For Ever Step 1 Skin Equalizer** before I apply my foundation; it makes my skin feel so soft and satiny, as well as giving a gentle blurred effect to my make-up.

FOUNDATION

I love experimenting with different foundations, but I'm currently using **Make Up For Ever's Ultra HD Invisible Cover Foundation** in shade 'Y225 Marble', applying it with a foundation brush by **Zoeva**, the **102 Silk Finish**, that smooths down the foundation without leaving any brush marks for a really silky, creamy finish. I also like applying foundation with a Beauty Blender.

CONTOURING

For contouring I generally use powder products such as the **Anastasia Beverly Hills Contour Kit**, the **Kat Von D Shade + Light Face Contour Palette** or the **Rodial Instaglam Compact Deluxe Contouring Powder**. If I want a more defined contour, I will use a cream contour before applying my powder contour, and for this I will use something like the

Amazing Cosmetics Perfection Stick in 'Deep'.

COMPLEXION

Having a good skincare routine is essential because your skin is the base for everything to be applied onto. How you prep your skin before making it up makes all the difference. I couldn't live without a cleanser, toner and moisturiser. At night I also like applying an oil too.

I am currently using:

Sunday Riley Ceramic Slip Clay Cleanser, or **Liz Earle Cleanse and Polish**™ **Hot Cloth Cleanser**

Kiehl's Creamy Eye Treatment with Avocado Pixi Glow Tonic

Liz Earle Toner

Kiehl's Ultra Facial Cream

Kiehl's Midnight Recovery

By Terry Liftessence Eye Contour

Concentrate (at night only, along with the other steps but before moisturiser)

I also love spritzing on **Caudalie's Beauty Elixir** to freshen me up throughout the day for an extra glow.

CONCEALER

I use a great product by **Maybelline** called **Age Rewind** in 'Light'.

DEFINITION

When it comes to definition, there are a few general products that I would pick out.

Darker shades of eyeshadow – I blend this into the crease of the eyelid, as it creates real depth and definition.

When I want my lips to stand out, I make sure I use a liner. It's always a good idea if you are wearing a strongly coloured lipstick – it will give your pout a nicely defined shape.

For defined cheekbones and facial structure, I would recommend the contouring products above.

BLUSH

I like a range of blush products and shades, from pinks and nudes for a fresh finish, to warmer and deeper tones for a bronzed look. My favourites are **Urban Decay Afterglow Blush** in 'Indecent' or 'Score', **Too Faced Love Flush** in

'Love Hangover' and **Marc Jacobs Shameless Bold Blush** in 'Reckless'.

HIGHLIGHT

My current favourite is by **Make Up For Ever** in the shade 'Rose Gold'. It's so pretty.

I often finish a look with **Laura Mercier Secret Brightening Powder** too. **Anastasia Beverly Hills Glow Kits** are also fab!

BLEND

Good blending is all about the application, whether that's done by hand, with a brush or sponge.

The **Sigma E40** brush is one I cannot live without. It is large and fluffy, so blends out your transition eyeshadow colours seamlessly through the crease. I also love the **Sigma E25**, which is a smaller blending brush. As it is smaller, it is better than the E40 at keeping the product in a precise area. To blend my concealer, I love using a damp **Beauty Blender**. I also use a **stippling brush** from the brand Furless to diffuse my contour, blush and highlight to avoid any layering lines.

TOOLKIT

This is a list of everything I have in my beauty toolkit – it covers every eventuality of my make-up needs!

Zoeva 102 Silk Finish Brush for foundation

Beauty Blender for foundation and concealer

MAC 266 Small Angle Brush for brows

Spooly to brush the brows

Real Techniques Setting Brush to apply the powder to set my concealer under my eyes

Benefit Hoola Bronzer Brush

Nars ITA Contour Brush

Morphe M501 Pro Pointed Blender Brush for highlighting my cheekbones

Real Techniques Blush Brush

Furless Stippling Brush PRO6F to blend my contour, blush and highlighter

Sigma E40 Blending Brush – large fluffy brush to blend my eyeshadows

Sigma E25 Blending Brush – smaller fluffy brush to blend eyeshadow

MAC 242 Shader Brush – use for shades on the base of the lid, good for shimmers/metallics

Morphe M507 Pointed Mini Blender Brush – a very small eyeshadow brush to add precise definition to the crease

Sigma E30 Pencil Brush – good for applying eyeshadow to the lower lash line

Sigma F75 Concealer Brush – to highlight cupid's bow, bridge of nose, brow bone and inner corner of the eye

GLOSS

I don't often wear gloss, but when I do I like the **Buxom Full-On™ Lip Polish (Shimmer Finish) Leah – Pink Champagne,** or **Butter Cream** from **Gerard Cosmetics.**

EYES

I love a warm, smoky eye and often use brands such as **Urban Decay (Naked Ultimate Basics Eyeshadow Palette)** or the **Anastasia Beverly Hills Modern Renaissance Eye Shadow Palette.**

From the Anastasia palette, I start off with 'Golden Ochre', using an **E40 fluffy brush** to apply the shadow at the top of my eyelid crease, using circular motions and windshield-wiper motions to blend it in. Then I build things up with 'Raw Sienna' in the same place, adding 'Burnt Orange' through the crease using the same brush, merging everything together. Using a smaller **E25 brush**, which I position using my teeth, I add 'Venetian Red' on the outer corner of my lid and run that through the crease as well to add definition.

For a strong line of eyeliner, I like **Kat Von D Tattoo Liner** in black. I find this the easiest liner to use because it looks like a felt tip but it is smooth, because it is made up of hundreds of small hairs so it glides on effortlessly.

BRONZER

My preferred product is **Benefit Hoola Bronzing Powder**, although I change it up quite regularly. However, I feel Hoola is a shade a lot of different skin tones can wear, so it's a great all-rounder.

HAIR

I like to take good care of my hair and make sure it is nicely styled. To do this, I use a detangling product before blow-drying to ensure all knots are out, and I always use a heat protector spray before applying any kind of heat to my hair. I also use a serum or oil to make sure my ends are super-soft.

When it comes to styling, I use my trusty **ghd**s to curl or straighten my hair. If it's curled, I finish it with the **Charles Worthington Volume & Bounce Texturising Spray**; if it's straight, I sometimes spritz over a shine spray for extra sleekness.

LIPS

I used to wear a lot of pink lipstick, but I'm more of a nude type of girl now. My current faves are **Anastasia Beverly Hills Liquid Lipstick** in 'Pure Hollywood' and **Too Faced Melted Matte Liquified Matte Lipstick** in 'Child Star'. I also love wearing **Too Faced Perfect Lips** lip liner in the shade 'Perfect Nude' with either **Tom Ford Lip Color** in 'Nude Vanille' or **Gerard Cosmetics** lipstick in 'Kimchi Doll'.

For a strong red lip, my go-to shade at the moment is **Too Faced Melted Matte Liquified Matte Lipstick** in 'Lady Balls'.

BROWS

I use **Anastasia Dipbrow Pomade** in 'Taupe', applied with a **MAC 266** brush, along with **Illamasqua Brow Build** or **Anastasia Beverly Hills Clear Brow Gel** (this keeps the brows in place and adds texture).

BOMBSHELL

These are the products I use to create my bombshell look:

Primer: **Too Faced Hangover Replenishing Face Primer**

Foundation: **NARS Sheer Glow Foundation** in 'Punjab'

Concealer: **Maybelline Age Rewind,** set by powder from the **Kat Von D Shade + Light Face Contour Palette**

Highlight: 'Peaceful' from the **Individual Blush Collection** by **Sigma**

Blush: Born-To from the **Individual Blush Collection** by Sigma

Eyeshadow: Using warm colours from the **Morphe Jaclyn Hill Favorites Palette,** I apply with the **E40 brush** from **Sigma**

Liquid eyeliner: I like **MAC Liquid Eye Liner** in 'Boot Black' for this look, but any make will do

Pencil liner: I use **MAC Eye Kohl** in 'Smolder'

Mascara: **Benefit Roller Girl Roller Lash**

Lipstick: **Gerard Cosmetics Lipstick** in 'Kimchi Doll'

Gloss: **Sigma Lip Vex** in 'Chill Out'

RADIANCE

When I want to give my hair an extra boost, I have used **Kylie Jenner Bellami Hair Kouture Extensions.** You can wear them curly or straight. I thought they were amazing (I had loads of compliments wearing them!).

SKINCARE

I have a specific skincare routine that I run through every morning and evening. These are the products that I keep coming back to time and time again:

Liz Earle Instant Boost™ Skin Tonic Spritzer
Kiehl's Midnight Recovery Eye
Liz Earle Skin Repair™ Moisturiser for normal to combination skin
Liz Earle Superskin™ Concentrate For Night
Estée Lauder Advanced Night Repair Eye Serum